PONDERING(S)

PONDERING(S)

Thoughts on:
Consecration · Worship
Presence · Discipleship

WAYNE BERRY

WordCrafts

Pondering(s)
Copyright © 2016
Wayne Berry

Cover design by David Warren.

All rights reserved. No part of this book may be reproduced, stored in a retrieval system, or transmitted in any form or by any means – electronic, mechanical, photocopy, recording, or otherwise – without the prior written permission of the publisher. The only exception is brief quotations for review purposes.

Unless otherwise noted all Scripture quotations are taken from the New American Standard Bible ® (NASB), Copyright © 1960, 1962, 1963, 1968, 1971, 1972, 1973, 1975, 1977, 1995 by The Lockman Foundation. Used by permission. www.Lockman.org

Scripture quotations marked (The Message) taken from THE MESSAGE. Copyright © by Eugene H. Peterson 1993, 1994, 1995, 1996, 2000, 2001, 2002. Used by permission of NavPress. All rights reserved. Represented by Tyndale House Publishers, Inc.

Scripture quotations marked (KJV) taken from the King James Version of the Bible, public domain.

All references to (Strong's) refer to *Strong's Exhaustive Concordance of the Bible*, public domain.

PACING THE CAGE and LOVER IN A DANGEROUS TIME
Written by Bruce Cockburn
Used by permission of Rotten Kiddies Music LLC

HEAVEN ON EARTH
Written by David Binion, Joshua Dufrene, John Brockman
Used by permission of Capitol CMG

HOLY SPIRIT
Written by Bryan and Katie Torwalt
Used by permission of Capitol CMG

Published by WordCrafts Press
Buffalo, Wyoming 82834
www.wordcrafts.net

CONTENTS

PREFACE i
INTRODUCTION vi
CHAPTER 1 - Pondering Consecration 1
CHAPTER 2 - Pondering Worship 24
CHAPTER 3 - Pondering Presence 55
CHAPTER 4 - Pondering Discipleship 92
EPILOGUE 115
IN REMEMBRANCE... 116

PREFACE

In this digital daze we live in, pondering is virtually becoming a lost art. The pace of the planet keeps pulling us along at a speed that few can keep up with. The rapid changes in technology, social values, and cultural processing seem to be forcing us to spend more time trying to adjust to changes than to consider them in any real detail and depth. If the so-called advancements to humanity continue at their current rate, thinking may become obsolete. It has already become optional for millions of people.

> *"Turn and face the strange changes."*
> ~D. Bowie

Pondering links to meditation; meditation links to contemplation; and contemplation links to thinking. Each of those terms has at its base the principle of thinking things through - giving our attention through thought.

> *"Look up, and be alert to what is going on around Christ - that's where the action is. See things from His perspective."*
> ~Colossians 3:3
> (The Message)

PONDERING(S)

*"Cease striving and know that I God:
I will be exalted among the nations,
I will be exalted in the earth."*

~Psalm 46:10
(NASB)

PREFACE

SET YOUR SIGHTS ABOVE
(Colossians 3:1-3)

Set your *affection on things above,
and not on earthly things
For you are dead,
and your life is hidden with Christ, in God

So brothers be thankful,
and let His Word dwell in your hearts with love
Share with each other, take care of each other,
and set your sights above

If you are risen with Christ, our Savior,
then He is your all in all
And the peace of God, dwelling in your hearts,
is the peace to which you're called

So sisters be thankful,
and let His Word dwell in your hearts with love
Whatever you do, let His Spirit show through,
and set your sights above

Learn charity through faithfulness,
doing all for Christ, our King
Giving praise to God with gratefulness,
bringing honor to His name

(W. Berry, See and Say Songs, BMI)

*Affection (Mind / KJV) – To exercise the mind. To be mentally disposed (in a certain direction). To interest oneself in (with concern or obedience). To care for or about. From a word meaning *cognitive understanding*.

PONDERING(S)

> *"Heaven is calling for you to come higher*
> *To see everything from a new point of view*
> *To be seated with Jesus in heavenly places*
> *From His perspective everything is made new"*
> (David Binion, Joshua Dufrene, John Brockman)

The Bible provides a considerable amount of information regarding how our minds should be actively engaged in matters related to the consideration of Scriptures, and also to how we are to live our lives based on what we learn.

> *"People with their minds set on You, You will keep completely whole, steady on their feet, because they keep at it and don't quit. Depend on God and keep at it because in the Lord God you have a sure thing."*
>
> ~Isaiah 26:3-4
> (The Message)

> *"Love the Lord your God with all your passion and prayer and intelligence…"*
> ~Matthew 22:37/Mark 12:30/Luke 10:27
> (The Message)

{Also see Romans 7:25, 12:2; 2 Corinthians 8:12; Ephesians 4:23; Hebrews 8:10; 1 Peter 1:13}

> *"One of the things that has happened in the last hundred and a few more years is that society, through its institutions, has very carefully taken Christ's teachings and set them out of the domain of knowledge and put them in an area called faith. That shift has deprived faith of its power, because faith is never meant to exist apart from knowledge, where knowledge is possible. What is possible*

PREFACE

through the Scriptures and the actions of God in history is knowledge — knowledge of God, knowledge of human life — and that dignity has to be restored."

~D. Willard

"Place your hand on your forehead, and say, 'engage.'"

~Bishop Tudor Bismark

INTRODUCTION

I am a teaching Levite. That's part of what I'm called to do in service for my Lord by serving His people. I base that comment on two things – Scripture and experience.

> *"He gave the priest detailed instructions and encouraged them in the work of leading worship in The Temple of God. He also told the Levites who were in charge of *teaching and guiding Israel in all matters of worship (they were especially consecrated for this)."*
>
> ~2 Chronicles 35:2-3
> (The Message)

*Teaching (from Strong's Concordance) – To separate mentally; to consider or understand; to inform; to cause to discern.

This manuscript is a sacrificial offering of worship intended to bring honor and glory to the Father, Son, and Holy Ghost (Colossians 3:17). It is my hope that in some way it will be used to advance the Kingdom of God.

Although it's entitled **Pondering(s)** it's not really addressing *pondering*, as such. I've already briefly addressed

INTRODUCTION

the meaning of pondering in the preface. The focus of each chapter will be on four specific personal ponderings:

Consecration / Worship / Presence / Discipleship

I am purposed to try and share some of the insights the Lord has given me regarding each of those topics. I consider all four of them as stepping stones for me personally as they relate to how I've continued to walk out my faith through "a long obedience in the same direction" as Eugene Peterson once said, quoting (of all people) Friedrich Nietzsche.

I believe that my relationship to/with the Lord, Christ Jesus, requires me to try and develop a personal theology that I can hold to, testify to, and live out (1 Peter 3:15 - The Message). For the most part, what you'll read on the pages that follow will be based on what I see, what I believe, and what I'm still trying to understand in regards to the four specific subjects of my pondering.

I've attempted to present my thoughts as clearly as possible because it's important to me that I'm understood. I hope you'll be able to get on, and stay on, the same page with me throughout this manuscript. However, I'm not too concerned with whether you agree with me or not regarding what I have to say. I'm not seeking for unity of agreement. For the most part, I'm only concerned about unity of understanding. Here's why:

There are many highways leading up to Zion (Psalm 84:5 - NASB). There are also many wells to draw up from along the way (Isaiah 12:3). The #1 priority should be that we are headed in the same direction.

> *"There is one body and one Spirit, just as also you were called in one hope of your calling: one Lord,*

PONDERING(S)

one faith, one baptism, one God and Father of all who is over all and through all and in all."

~Ephesians 4:3-4
(NASB)

How blessed are those whose strength is in You, in whose hearts are the highway(s) to Zion!

Passing through the valley of Baca they make it a place of springs; the early rain also covers it with blessings. They go from strength to strength until every one of them appears before God in Zion."

~Psalm 84:5-7
(NASB)

INTRODUCTION

WELLS OF SALVATION
(Isaiah 12:3)

*"With joy will I draw water
Out of the wells of salvation
This is the day I will say, 'Praise the Lord'
My God is the Rock on which I stand
He rescued me from a barren land
This is the day I will say, 'Praise the Lord'"*
　　　　　　　　　(W. Berry, See and Say Songs, BMI)

PONDERING(S)

Consider this a handbook of sorts to use as a guide on the roadway you're currently traveling. As they say in Africa, *Journey mercies. Go well, be well* (an old African blessing).

> *"My left foot says, 'Glory,' and my right foot says, 'Amen.'"*
>
> ~Annie Dillard

CHAPTER 1
Pondering Consecration

Some twenty or so years ago I had the honor of studying under the direction of Professor Robert Weber at the Institute for Worship Studies. As a student I picked up a teaching tool from him that has served me well over the years. Often in his classes, he used what he called a "working definition" when he wanted his students to focus in on a certain word or topic. Here's how it worked:

He would explain to the class that he wanted everyone to consider his "working definition" as a point of agreement in terms of understanding or belief. He didn't care if the students had a different idea of their own (in terms of meaning), nor did he necessarily intend for them to believe as he did. However, for the sake of a unified understanding, he encouraged the students to accept his "working definition" in order to move everyone along together as he taught. That being said, here's my "working definition" for *consecration*:

{**Consecration is the setting apart of any person, place or thing for acts of holy service.**}

PONDERING(S)

The ponderings to follow will all be unpacked out of that definition. So, let's begin.

The first thing I have to say about how the process of consecration works is that we must begin by determining what acts of holy service are. Why? Because you cannot consecrate acts of unholy service. Doing so would be a contradiction in terms. I suppose you could approach this by saying that you'd first have to determine what unholy acts are, and then not do them. Otherwise, the very act of consecration would be compromised. Are you tracking what I'm saying here?

If not, perhaps you should allow yourself a little pondering space while you read what I've just said again. Having a grasp on this first point will have a direct bearing on what follows in this chapter.

The best example of consecration from my personal point of view would be what takes place when someone surrenders their life to Christ by accepting Him as Savior. When that happens, almost everyone who comes to salvation prays a prayer which basically says something like, "I give my life to you, Lord." We then receive reconciliation through our initial act of consecration, and the saving *grace of God (Ephesians 2:8). Even if we've never heard the word or understood the concept, what we have done is to set ourselves apart for holy service to God, through Christ's Spirit, which is, by definition, exactly what it means to be consecrated.

*Grace is the empowering Presence of God, enabling me to be who He created me to be, so I can do what He calls me to do.

However, that formative first step of consecration isn't all there is to living a consecrated life (or lifestyle). Step one births you into God's Kingdom, but it doesn't grow you up into it. There are many more steps ahead we are called to take regarding consecration before we reach a level of spiritual maturity in matters of service unto our Lord (see Ephesians 4:15; 1 Peter 2:2; 2 Peter 3:18).

I'm going to continue opening up an understanding for you about this process. But, for the sake of clarity, I'd like you to consider a particular aspect of how the use of biblical language can sometimes be confusing.

In the KJV (and a few other translations) the words *sanctification* and *consecration* are sometimes interchangeable. On occasion one word can be used instead of the other, and vice versa. That can be confusing if you haven't worked with both topics as distinct from one another. Having handled both topics for several years of study, and practical application, I have no problem or issue with how the words are interchanged – because I see a difference, and I understand how that difference can (or should) be considered. Let me explain by using a scriptural example:

In Joshua 3:5 we read that Joshua is giving the wilderness children a directive to follow. He says to the people, *"consecrate yourselves, for tomorrow the Lord will do wonders among you."*

> *"For God Himself works on our souls, in their deepest depths, taking increasing control as we are progressively willing to be prepared for His wonder."*
>
> ~T. Kelly

Clearly that verse is placing the responsibility upon the people to set themselves apart. To do so requires something of them on an individual and personal level. The holy service that Joshua is calling the people to offer is meant to prompt them to make themselves available to God. Therefore, you could say that consecration was their work in the context of that verse. Thereafter as believers – on a personal level - it becomes our work too, if we are purposed and intentional about offering ourselves to God through our own act(s) of consecration.

On the other hand, we find that the principle or practice of sanctification in the New Testament is the work of the Holy Spirit (1 Peter 1:2). Such a process empowered by and implemented through the Holy Spirit is the very process by which He conforms us into the character, nature, and personality of our Lord, Christ Jesus. The Spirit does the work we cannot do ourselves. We cannot convert or conform our own lives into the likeness of our Savior, for that is one of the major roles the Spirit is here to do. I'll say it this way:

The Holy Spirit sanctifies what we give Him to sanctify through our personal and individual act(s) of consecration. The two roles work in conjunction with each other and they are (in a biblical sense) necessary for the process to work properly. We do our work, and the Spirit does His. Consider all that from this perspective: *"Therefore humble yourselves under the mighty hand of God, the He may exalt you at the proper time..."* (1 Peter 5:6a). It is our job to humble ourselves through the process and practice of consecration. It is God's job, through the Spirit, and at His will, to exalt us (1 Thessalonians 4:3). If we insist on doing God's job, then He has no choice but to do ours.

{Selah...pause and ponder}

To further clarify what I'm saying, consider this:

In the KJV, Joshua 3:5 uses the word sanctify instead of consecrate. That's where the language can get confusing.

If consecration is our job (as Joshua clearly states that it is), then how are we to sanctify ourselves since the New Testament clearly states that to be the work of the Holy Spirit? You may not agree with my theological approach in this matter. But, in order to proceed from here, I encourage you to withhold any judgment that may put you at odds with me until I develop my thoughts further.

Ready or Not:

Let's look at the Joshua 3:5 verse with a little more attention to the details it provides us:

Joshua tells the people to consecrate themselves in preparation for the wonders God is going to do the following day – tomorrow. So, when are the people to perform their act(s) of consecration? The answer to that is found in a word that isn't in the text, but is nonetheless implied in it. The verse could/should read, *"Consecrate yourselves (today), for tomorrow God will do wonders among you."* The actions required in order for consecration to be in place are to take place *prior* to the need for them to be established. Joshua is saying that God's movement among the people (His awesome deeds) are going to take place tomorrow - *after* the people have consecrated themselves. I take that to mean that not being spiritually prepared for God to move prior to Him doing so has a direct bearing on how available a person or persons are to being in on the action when He starts to move. In other words, the lack of consecration in a believer's life can have a direct bearing on how available they are to take part in acts of holy service. Their ability to get in on a move of God then becomes limited. We can miss out on at least some portion of God's Presence, power, and purpose as He moves if we are not first prepared spiritually for such movement when it begins.

I would call that a lack of consecration, wouldn't you?

There are theological exceptions to the practice of consecration being solely our responsibility. However, the exception doesn't cancel out someone's individual or personal obligation of putting the process to work. No. Rather, it merely modifies it. I'll show you what I mean by looking at Jeremiah 1:5 which says, *"Before I formed you in the womb I knew you, and before you were born I consecrated you…"*

In that verse we see that Jehovah is in fact the one doing the consecrating. You could say that He is the Consecrator – for that He is.

So, that does offer us a view for a modified manner of consecration taking place. The modification being that someone other than ourselves can set us apart for acts of holy service. However, the fulfillment of such an action (by someone other than us) does not complete the process. If we are not willing to walk in and serve out of an act of consecration spoken over us, or to us, then the process is short circuited altogether. **We are never exempt from following through with the responsibility placed upon us in matters related to yielded and obedient service.** The entire process places two specific questions before us which we alone must answer:

1. Are we willing and available to present ourselves through acts of consecration which we do of our own free will?
2. Are we willing and available to carry out our own acts of consecration when someone in authority places a charge (calling) on or over us?

Answering both those questions in the affirmative enables us to be available to serve God's Kingdom in whatever ways He may call us to. Answering either one of them with a "No" can or will block our availability to willingly co-operate with what God is doing, and when He's doing it. I personally view the entire subject of consecration as being one of the most basic, yet overlooked, misunderstood, and rarely taught on or preached about subjects within the church today.

Here's an example which applies in the world we live in daily, where the rubber meets the road so to speak: This metaphor uses an automobile, which many people have access to. A car is a thing. You drive it to places. When you drive it, you are in it, and you are a person. So, there is a person, a place and a thing involved.

Let's say that you have consecrated yourself and your car for acts of holy service. If that were the case, then would you also consecrate the places you drive to, and also the manner in which you drive (speed limit, consideration of others, safety issues, etc.)? Perhaps this perspective will help you see why I say that every aspect of a Christian's life is potentially included in the consecration process. Try plugging any person, place, or thing into the equation and you begin to understand just how deep and wide this concept really is.

Here's another example from Scripture that provides us with an even clearer look into how this process of consecration is meant to work:

Go to 2 Chronicles 29 in your translation of choice and read the entire chapter, then we'll examine it together.

Go read; I'll wait here…

I'll make two observations before our examination begins: Firstly, I consider this chapter to be the best example of how the process of consecration should work. Secondly, learning how to apply what it teaches regarding obedience and servanthood can be life changing in terms of our relationship to the Father, Son, and Holy Ghost.

In verse 3, we are given the context for what's about to take place. Hezekiah passes down a directive to begin a refurbishing of the "house of the Lord." If you'll recall the "working definition" I mentioned earlier, it contained 3 areas of consideration for consecration: Person / Place / Thing. Clearly the "house of the Lord" is a place. So, what's being addressed is how to take the necessary steps for consecration by setting it apart for holy service.

In verse 4, Hezekiah assigns two groups of people to carry out his wishes – Priests and Levites. These two groups are chosen because they are (or should be) properly trained (discipled) and equipped to serve. They not only have a historical foundation for doing so, they also understand the principles and the precepts of living a consecrated life in service before and unto the Lord. Their spiritual heritage and their way of living have positioned them to conduct the works of service they are now charged with.

In verses 5 through 19, we see the specific details of what is needed to be done in order to restore the Temple to a place made holy and pure for ministry.

Note that the work that's described has to do with the things "in the house" as well as the house itself. At this point in the narrative, the process of being consecrated now has a *place* as well as the *things* in it. I draw your attention back to what Joshua told the people would take place after they prepared themselves through consecration. He stated that God would "do wonders." In Strong's Concordance, *wonders* is defined as: being separated or distinguished; to make great or wonderful; to arise in order to accomplish; to do marvelous things (i.e. miracles).

The point of setting apart any person, place, or thing

for holy service is to prepare them to be able and available for service if/when the need arises.

{Simply stated, consecration is a biblical way of preparing to serve.}

As we look a little deeper into the chapter, we will see exactly how such preparation enables holy service to take place. We will also see what can happen when the process has not been followed properly.

Picking up the narrative again in verse 19 we're told that *"all the utensils which King Ahaz had discarded during his reign in his unfaithfulness, we have prepared and consecrated; and behold, they are before the altar of the Lord."*

Thereafter, in verses 20-30 we see a listing of what took place once everything had (apparently) been restored for proper use. As you read through this list, you'll see that a worship service is in formation. The liturgical dynamics we're shown are happening in a congregational setting. There is an order of worship being followed in detail, with nothing being overlooked. However, as it turns out, that's not really the case. For something happens beginning in verse 34 that introduces us to the very thing I've been trying to get to. Follow closely:

It had been years since a service of worship had been convened and the priests had become less than conscientious in their personal acts of consecration. So, when the need arose for them to serve they were not properly prepared. That in turn disqualified them from being a part (or taking part) in any God-wonders that might begin to transpire. They didn't lose their priesthood, but they did miss a profound and powerful moment to serve. The resolution to this problem is stated in verses 34 and 35.

> *"But the priests were too few, so that they were unable to skin all the burnt offerings; therefore their brothers the Levites helped them until the work was completed and until the other priests had consecrated themselves. For the Levites were more conscientious to consecrate themselves than the priests. There were also many burnt offerings with the fat of the peace offerings and with the libations for the burnt offerings. Thus the service of the house of the Lord was established again."*
>
> ~2 Chronicles 29:34-35
> (NASB)

Covenant Consecration:

Up to this point I've basically been addressing consecration in the context of process – how it works and what it means. However, the underpinning for that process (biblically speaking) is the establishment of a covenant. The outworking of consecrated actions is built upon the intent of the acts themselves – and that intent is based on covenant. The *why* of a covenant is where the *what* and *how* of consecration come from. Covenant is the foundation upon which the principle of consecration is built.

The subject of covenant is very broad and deep in Scripture. There are many types to consider, each having its own varied components and usages. I am not qualified to explain them all. I don't have the theological knowledge to do so, nor is there a need to do so in reference to what I'm presenting here. For the sake of the subject matter in this chapter, I will focus on what I call a "worship covenant" by providing the insight that the Spirit has given me. I'll be drawing from Nehemiah chapters 8-13 for my source material. What follows has been culled from those chapters.

The covenant being considered in those chapters has at its core four basic components: Name / Place / Protection / Provision. Here's how they are applied when a covenant is being entered into:

1. A people who have no *name* (covering) take on the name of someone with authority to rule over them. In other words, they become subjects under that leader's rule.
2. A people who have no *place* (homeland or property) of their own are given a place to dwell that belongs to the ruler. The ownership is retained by the authority over them, but they are allowed to oversee it as if it were their own through their stewardship.
3. A people with no means of *protection* to defend themselves, having no armaments or army, come under the watch-care of the authority who maintains and controls the warriors to use them.
4. A people with no *provision* to sustain themselves by growing food is given the resources (seed, livestock, farming tools, etc.) in order to plant, nurture, and harvest what they'll need in order to live.

As Christians, we share in each of those four areas through our relationship with God, in Jesus, empowered by the Holy Spirit. Here's how:

We, a people with no name, come under the authority and covering of the Sovereign Ruler when we take Christ as our namesake (i.e. Christian). We are born into this world with no property or place of our own (Psalm 24:1). When we unite ourselves under the government of the Kingdom of God, we are given a place to dwell and establish our lives upon (Psalm 16:5-6). We, as Kingdom citizens, are protected and defended by the holy hosts of angels and supernatural-spiritual- warriors directly under the charge of God-Of-The-Angel-Armies (Psalm 91:1-4). Jehovah is the Lord of hosts and our security is found in His strength (Psalm 24:8) and under His sheltering wings (Psalm 61:1-4). And, we are sustained with daily bread given us by the ongoing manifestation of His grace, mercy, and sustaining power.

> *"In Him we live and move and have our being"*
> ~Acts 17:28
> (NASB)

These overall resources are poured directly into our lives once we have established covenant with the One True God. When we yield ourselves in obedient service (consecration) to Him, this becomes our inherited lifestyle. As we live committed to the commandment of Deuteronomy 5:7, *"You shall have no other gods before Me,"* we are given a Divine guarantee of His name, place, protection, and provision.

> *"All our springs of joy are in You"*
> ~Psalm 87:7b
> (NASB)

However, the question of priority arises if/when we fail to remain yielded and obedient in our loyalty and service to Father God. Consider this:

There is an alternate translation of Deuteronomy 5:7 which provides a much broader explanation of what's being required of us as subjects of our King and His Kingdom rule. In the margin of the NASB an alternative reading is,

CONSECRATION

"You shall have no other gods (besides) Me." Understood that way, there is a difference between having only one God who comes before other gods. The difference is that we are called to have no other gods at all - period. You see, the text clearly states that there are other gods (small g and plural). Meaning that there are in fact other gods, but they are not The God! When the text is read as having no other gods *besides* God, then what it's saying is that we are to live with only One God as our God.

We are to have no lesser gods (little g) in our lives to divide our loyalties, diminish our service, distract our attention, and weaken our relational bonds of fellowship and intimacy.

> *"Their gods are metal and wood, handmade in a basement shop: Carved mouths that can't talk, painted eyes that can't see, tin ears that can't hear, molded noses that can't smell, hands that can't grasp, feet that can't walk or run, throats that never utter a sound. Those who make them have become just like them, have become just like the gods they trust."*
>
> ~Psalm 115:4-8
> (The Message)

PONDERING(S)

NO OTHER GOD
(Deuteronomy 5:7)

No other god can claim the place You know
in my heart

No other god can break the bond You hold
to my heart

All the praise I have, I offer up to You,
in worship of the Most High God

No other god can speak the words of life
to my soul
No other god can sweep away the night
dark glow

All the praise I have, I offer up to You,
in worship of the Most High God

You are Holy, and worthy of all praise,
You are Righteous, and just in all Your ways,
You are Faithful, Compassionate and True,
God Almighty, I yield myself to You

All the praise I have, I offer up to You,
in worship of the Most High God
(W. Berry, See and Say Songs, BMI)

We can see the outworking of this in the New Testament where Jesus states that, *"...true worshipers will worship the Father in spirit and truth"* (John 4:23a). When that statement is considered in light of Deuteronomy 5:7 it can be understood as saying this:

All human beings ever born, living now, or yet to be born are worshipers of someone, or something. However, from among all those who have the potential and propensity of worshiping other gods (little g), the Father is seeking for *specific* worshipers who will only worship Him. That's what it means to have no other gods (little g) BESIDES One.

{Selah...pause and ponder}

Any time there is a breakdown in a believer's singular honoring of this "One God" principle, the possibility of a broken covenant can take place. I believe that to be the situation in the lives of many "born again" believers. When covenant has been broken it becomes necessary to reestablish a bond of unity between us and our Sovereign. With some prayerful and studied reading, a means of reestablishment or reconnection can be found in the chapters 8-13 of Nehemiah.

A Biblical Protocol for Reestablishing Covenant:

Conviction – From the Word and/or through the Holy Spirit

Confession – To God (vertically), and/or to others (horizontally when necessary)

Repentance – Changing the way we're thinking / Turning away from unrighteousness

Restoration/Renewal – Being repositioned to an upright place and thereafter being refashioned in any necessary areas (i.e. sanctification through the Spirit)

Celebration – Praise, adoration, and exaltation for having been restored and renewed

Worship Evangelism – Our witness through covenant consecration enables the power and purity of our testimony to resound into the world

Revival – Our worship begins to serve as a tool of evangelism drawing others into the process of covenant consecration (salvation and its outworking)

A Scriptural Outworking of Covenant Reestablishment:

Psalm 51 is a perfect example of how repentance leads to restoration of what's been broken, discarded, or lost in a relationship with the Lord. In it we see the protocol mentioned above at work in David's spiritual walk. Let's talk a look:

Conviction – The Holy Spirit uses the prophet Nathan to expose David's sin thereby bringing him to the point of conviction. David has not lost His relationship with the Lord. However, his ability to present himself for ongoing holy service (consecration) has been damaged deeply and is in need of some major repair work.

Confession – Verses 1-12 show us David's vertical act of confession unto the Lord. He is quite specific in his confession when he addresses individual areas of violation regarding to living righteously. He admits to: Sin / Transgressions / Iniquity.

Each has its own characteristics of failure in relationship to how consecrated he can be in carrying out his service.

Transgression – To break away from just authority. To trespass, quarrel, offend, or rebel against cultural, moral, or spiritual laws.

Iniquity – To cover up or hide. Often a sin pattern passed down from generation to generation. A habitual returning to unrighteousness.

Sin – An offense; offender; to be led astray; to commit harm or cause loss.

Much can be learned from how David moves to reposition himself in humility in order to receive forgiveness and purification. The more detailed the prayers of confession, the more complete the next step of repentance will be.

Repentance + Restoration/Renewal – Verses 13 and 14 place David at the very opening where his restoration can begin in full. He acknowledges before the Lord that he understands that his confession can enable him to turn away from the wrong path he had wandered onto and reset his steps (and his thinking) to again realign as he moves into a reestablished covenant.

Celebration – Verse 15 shows us the beginning stage of praise release (by faith).

Worship Evangelism – Verses 16 and 17 begin to extend the resounding of worship out beyond David's life personally.

> *"I learned God-worship when my pride was shattered. Heart-shattered lives ready for love don't for a moment escape God's notice."*
>
> (The Message)

Revival – Verses 18 and 19 extend the reestablishment out beyond David's reach and into the lives who will be touched by it.

> *"Make Zion the place you delight in, repair Jerusalem's broken-down walls. Then you'll get real*

worship from us, acts of worship small and large, including all the bulls they can heave onto your altar!"

(The Message)

I'll begin closing out this chapter with quotes from Oswald Chambers. They are taken from the most widely read devotional book in history, *My Utmost for His Highest*.

January 26
Consecration is the act of continually separating myself from everything except that which God has appointed me to do. It is not a one-time experience but an ongoing process. Am I continually separating myself and looking to God every day of my life?

July 22
When I pray, "Lord, show me what sanctification means for me," He will show me. It means being made one with Jesus. Sanctification is not something Jesus puts in me — it is Himself in me (see 1 Corinthians 1:30).

July 23
Sanctification means the impartation of the holy qualities of Jesus Christ to me. It is the gift of His patience, love, holiness, faith, purity, and godliness that is exhibited in and through every sanctified soul. Sanctification is not drawing from Jesus the power to be holy — it is drawing from Jesus the very holiness that was exhibited in Him, and that He now exhibits in me. Sanctification is an impartation, not an imitation. Imitation is

something altogether different. The perfection of everything is in Jesus Christ, and the mystery of sanctification is that all the perfect qualities of Jesus are at my disposal. Consequently, I slowly but surely begin to live a life of inexpressible order, soundness, and holiness — "...kept by the power of God..." (1 Peter 1:5).

September 4

"If anyone comes to Me and does not hate his father and mother, wife and children, brothers and sisters, yes, and his own life also, he cannot be My disciple" (Luke 14:26). He was not saying that this person cannot be good and upright, but that he cannot be someone over whom Jesus can write the word Mine. Any one of the relationships our Lord mentions in this verse can compete with our relationship with Him. I may prefer to belong to my mother, or to my wife, or to myself, but if that is the case, then, Jesus said, "[You] cannot be My disciple." This does not mean that I will not be saved, but it does mean that I cannot be entirely His.

Our Lord makes His disciple His very own possession, becoming responsible for him. "...you shall be witnesses to Me..." (Acts 1:8). The desire that comes into a disciple is not one of doing anything for Jesus, but of being a perfect delight to Him. The missionary's secret is truly being able to say, "I am His, and He is accomplishing His work and His purposes through me. Be entirely His"!

September 30

We take our own spiritual consecration and try to make it into a call of God, but when we get right with Him He brushes all this aside. Then He gives us a tremendous, riveting pain to fasten our attention on something that we never even dreamed could be His call for us. And for one radiant, flashing moment we see His purpose, and we say, "Here am I! Send me" (Isaiah 6:8).

This call has nothing to do with personal sanctification, but with being made broken bread and poured-out wine. Yet God can never make us into wine if we object to the fingers He chooses to use to crush us. We say, "If God would only use His own fingers, and make me broken bread and poured-out wine in a special way, then I wouldn't object!" But when He uses someone we dislike, or some set of circumstances to which we said we would never submit, to crush us, then we object. Yet we must never try to choose the place of our own martyrdom. If we are ever going to be made into wine, we will have to be crushed—you cannot drink grapes. Grapes become wine only when they have been squeezed.

I wonder what finger and thumb God has been using to squeeze you? Have you been as hard as a marble and escaped? If you are not ripe yet, and if God had squeezed you anyway, the wine produced would have been remarkably bitter. To be a holy person means that the elements of our natural life experience the very Presence of God as they are providentially broken in His service. We have to be placed into God and brought into agreement with Him before we can be broken bread in His hands. Stay right with God and let Him do as He likes, and you will find that He is producing the kind of bread and wine that will benefit His other children.

There is a perspective regarding sanctification given to us in Scripture based on the dynamics that take place in and through the sacramental actions of Holy Communion. I've been trying to embrace and incorporate how it's outworked into my life for decades. I first heard this teaching from Henri Nouwen in a lecture he was giving. It's from a book of his entitled *Life of The Beloved*. The process is this:

Taken / Blessed / Broken / Given

First, we are taken (accepted into the Beloved) through redemption. Next, we are blessed abundantly through the Father's grace, mercy, and favor. Then, we are broken through the circumstances which He allows to take place in our lives (see Romans 8:28; James 1:2-4; 1 Peter 4:12). And, finally, we are given (passed around) as a form of spiritual sustenance to those we come into contact with. Much in the same way, Jesus said it was better for Him to leave in order for the Holy Spirit to come and take His place (John 16:7a). That happened in order that we could then become containers, or conduits of Divine Presence (1 Corinthians 3:16). The more broken we are in yielded service to the Father (in His hands), the more we are then able to be used (distributed) to those in need of the love, compassionate consideration, and the graciousness of reconciliation.

> *"Because of this decision we don't evaluate people by what they have or how they look. We looked at the Messiah that way once and got it all wrong, as you know. We certainly don't look at him that way anymore. Now we look inside, and what we see is that anyone united with the Messiah gets a fresh start, is created new. The old life is gone; a new life*

> *burgeons! Look at it! All this comes from the God who settled the relationship between us and him, and then called us to settle our relationships with each other. God put the world square with himself through the Messiah, giving the world a fresh start by offering forgiveness of sins. God has given us the task of telling everyone what he is doing. We're Christ's representatives. God uses us to persuade men and women to drop their differences and enter into God's work of making things right between them. We're speaking for Christ himself now: Become friends with God; he's already a friend with you. How? you ask. In Christ. God put the wrong on him who never did anything wrong, so we could be put right with God."*
>
> ~2 Corinthians 5:18-21
> (The Message)

The process of consecration, and the covenant that it is built upon, is vital in the life of every believer who desires to live in obedient service to the Lord. Being available in an ongoing intimate relationship with the Father, Son, and Holy Ghost is essential if we intend to participate (rather than spectate) in any move where the manifestations of God's Kingdom are taking place. Living our lives in that fashion provides a context for becoming a "living sacrifice" which is our service of worship (Romans 12:1 - NASB). That leads us to my next pondering focused on the subject of true, authentic, and biblical worship.

CONSECRATION

IN HIS HANDS

Your prayers are never yours alone
You offer them to God, and they become His own
And then He fashions them to fit into His perfect plan
Your prayers are not your own, once they're in His hands

Your dreams don't belong to you
They're part of Fathers heart, even when they don't come true
You have still been blessed to share
In things that He has planned
Your dreams are not your own once they're in His hands

Your life, it is a gift from God, ordered in His care
Through mercy, grace, and love
And when, and when you give your heart to Him
With all the praise you can
Your life becomes His own, once you're in His hands
                    (W. Berry, See and Say Songs, BMI)

CHAPTER 2
Pondering Worship

I'll begin this chapter with my "working definition" of worship:

Worship is the process by which the principles and precepts of God's Kingdom are worked into and out of the lives of believers in intimate relationship with the Father, Son, and Holy Ghost, through faithful obedience, sacrificial service, and personal and corporate offerings of adoration and exaltation.

Worship is a noun or a verb depending on how it is being communicated. It's a noun because it has form and substance – it is a thing. It is also a verb because it is something we do – requiring action (or better yet, engagement). According to Romans 12:1 it can be biblically understood as being part of everything we do (see the Message Bible).

Praise is the celebrative response to the God of the Kingdom, Christ Jesus (our blessed Savior), and the indwelling person of the Holy Spirit. If you'd like a scriptural basis for what I've said, try this one:

> *"Let every detail in your lives – words, actions, whatever – be done in the name of the Master, Jesus, thanking God the Father every step of the way."*
>
> ~Colossians 3:17
> (The Message)

Distinct Not Separate:

Worship and Praise are distinct, not separate. They are like two sides of the same coin so to speak. Let me develop that thought for you:

From Webster's Dictionary:

Separate: Solitary; set or kept apart; detached; not shared with another; individual.

Distinct: Distinguishable; things similar in effect by wholly in motive; presenting a clear, unmistakable impression.

The contemporary church today understands (or misunderstands) worship and praise as two separate things. To make matters worse theologically speaking, the current perception of each is that praise is offered up in our congregational gatherings using fast, up tempo songs - most often sung in the early portion of our services. Worship, on the other hand, presumably takes place among us when we are singing slower (and more emotionally sensitive) songs - sung closer to or just before the sermon takes place. Allow me just one brief moment to vent here: That is simply nonsense!

The first problem with that theological approach is that we are limiting both actions (praise and worship) to subjective expressions confined to personal experiences in the context of corporate gatherings. By doing so we compartmentalize them. Such expressed experiences are most certainly biblical in their outworking. But, they are really only components of a much larger concept. They are not the concept in total. To be scriptural, worship and praise should be considered (and integrated) into our lives and lifestyles together, not relegated to specific times in specific locations.

> *"Jesus said to her, "Woman, believe Me, an hour is coming when neither in this mountain nor in Jerusalem will you worship the Father."*
>
> ~John 4:21

The next problem - as I see it - is that by separating the two components, we uncouple them, when in fact they are not intended to be such. Here's why: When they are separated, over time they become aspects of our lives which cannot and do not take place together. They become sectioned off and categorized. Whereas, if they are perceived as being distinct (which is what they really are), then the interchange between them offers us the opportunity to experience and express them in a seamless flow of celebration, adoration, exaltation, awe and holy reverence.

Pastor Timothy Keller's comments provide a perspective of this idea of distinct instead of separate which can help explain what I'm saying. Writing about Psalm 95:1-4, he says, "This psalm and the next give us almost a liturgy for a service of gathered worship. The first stage is adoration. Let us rise up in joy to God the Creator (vs. 1-5). Let us praise Him for being the maker and sustainer of the world. *Worshiping is not always quiet and decorous. It can entail shouting, praising, leaping to our feet, singing out hearts out.* When the love of the immeasurably great and transcendent God of the universe becomes real to us, the joy should be uncontainable." Then continuing his insights with verses 5-7 he states, "The next element of worship is confession of our sin and need. *Let us bow down in humility to God the Redeemer (vs. 6, 7). In contrast to the exuberance of the first five verses, which fits with the postures of standing or even dancing, each of the three verbs in verse 6 have to do with getting low before God, since the Hebrew word for 'worship' here literally means to prostrate oneself.* We are to bow reverently, to kneel humbly before God, admitting our sinfulness and dependence. While adoration comes from seeing a God of glory, submission comes from seeing a God of grace, one who is our covenant God, who redeemed us and brought us as sheep into His fold (v.7)." Here you can clearly see that the components of praise and worship are interchangeable. As they both take place within the same Psalm, their outworking flows naturally from the heart of the Psalmist (see Hebrews 4:7) with no thought given to any aspects of what we now consider necessary in order to "enter in" to a "worship experience."

In The *Treasury of David*, Charles Spurgeon says of this same Psalm, "This is a Psalm of *invitation to worship*. It has a ring like church bells, and like the bells, it sounds *both merry and solemn*. At first it rings out a lively peal, and then it drops to a funeral knell, as if tolling at the funeral of the generation that perished in the wilderness. We will call it, 'The Psalm of the Provocation.'" Spurgeon goes on to say of verse one, "Let us sing with holy enthusiasm and make a sound that shows our earnestness. Let us lift our voices with abounding joy, actuated by that happy and peaceful spirit that trusting love is sure to foster." Then continuing, his commentary of verse two is, "We may come boldly into the immediate Presence of the Lord, for the Holy Spirit's voice in this Psalm invites us, but when we draw near, we should remember His great goodness and cheerfully confess it."

Such insights as these help to shed light on just how unified both aspects of adoration are biblically distinct, not separate. Worship and praise are not divided by fast songs – at the beginning of our corporate services, and slow songs setting an atmosphere for the sermon of the day. They belong together, like two sides of the same coin. Our worship isn't segregated internally, as we currently understand and practice it. It is integrated deep within our souls and includes each and every scriptural example that we can incorporate into our sacrificial offerings, both personally and corporately.

{We praise God with our worship, and we worship God when we praise.}

Our Father does not seek worship; He seeks worshipers. Worship is not merely something we do in meetings. It is a lifestyle or it simply is not worship. Worship is a spontaneous response to the Presence of God. If we would live our lives in awareness of the Presence of God we would always be worshiping. In corporate worship, worshipers gather to encourage one another and express their appreciation together. They are not enjoying worship; they are enjoying Father.

~F. Shults

My "go-to" Scripture concerning how this topic is manifested in a worshiper's life is in Psalm 63:3-7 which says this:

> *"Because Your lovingkindness is better than life, my lips will praise You (*shabach – to shout*).*

> *So I will bless (*barak – to bow in adoration*)
> You as long as I live; I will lift up my hands
> (*towah – to extend the hands in surrender*)
> in Your name. My soul is satisfied as with marrow
> and fatness, and my mouth offers praises (*halal –
> to jump for joy; to rave for God; to go wild
> with celebration*) with joyful lips. When I
> remember You on my bed, I meditate on You in the
> night watches, for You have been my help, and in
> the shadow of Your wings I sing for joy (*rana – to
> shout with abandon*)."*
> (NASB)

The dynamic expressions above are taking place as one overflowing sacrifice of emotion(s), moving back and forth, and in and out of a number of praise and worship components and postures all at the same time. What a beautifully incorporated view we are given here of a worshiper's intimate relationship of self-expression(s) to the Father, Son, and Holy Ghost. Would that we would adapt this example as our own – both personally and congregationally.

> *"A worshiper is one who is intimately acquainted with, and has a daily relationship with God exhibited through obedience."*
> ~John W. Stevenson

If it is our intention to live as *"true worshipers"* (John 4:24), then our worship is to be Trinitarian in nature and substance. We are called (commanded) to worship God the Father, Son, and Holy Ghost – the 3 in One. According to Scripture, and validated in church history, our "service of worship" (Romans 12:1, NASB) isn't to be offered separately to the three distinct persons of the Trinity.

Rather, it is to be inclusive – unified if you will – in terms of Who our worship is focused on, directed toward, and exalting of.

> *Praise God from Whom all blessings flow*
> *Praise Him all creatures here below*
> *Praise Him above ye heavenly hosts*
> *Praise Father, Son, and Holy Ghost*
>
> ~Thomas Ken
> "Doxology" (Public Domain)

> *"The God we worship is Trinitarian in nature - Father, Son and Holy Spirit - co-equal and, therefore each worthy of worship."*
>
> ~Polycarp to the Church in Smyrna, c. 100

> *"Wherefore also I praise you [God, the Father] for all things, I bless you, along with the everlasting and heavenly Jesus Christ, your beloved Son, with whom, to you and the Holy Spirit, be glory both now and to all coming ages. Amen"*
>
> ~Epistle from Smyrna, XIV

We keep messin' up how we understand and apply ourselves to the entire subject of worship by holding onto and continuing to repeat two basic theological misconceptions; that worship and praise are interchangeable terms and that worship is just about music. But,

1. Worship and praise are not separate things. They are distinct. Separating them not only weakens their Kingdom witness to the world-at-large, it also diminishes their impact on us personally in relationship to our sacrificial offerings.

2. Worship is not solely to be understood as having to do with music, songs, singing, and emotionally-experienced-expressions taking place in congregational gatherings. It isn't about location. It is about internal engagement (see Psalm 35:9-10a).

The longer we continue to allow those two misconceptions to define our theological perceptions of worship, the further away we'll move (wander) from a biblically based understanding of what it is intended to be. Whereas emotion, experience, dynamic expressions (personally and corporately) should be considered as part of our worship offering, they are only aspects of it. They are not the total substance of worship itself. Our understanding will never be truly biblical without a building-up-from-the-basics meaning of what worship is to be from a scriptural viewpoint.

There is a principle that is taught and often used in the study of the Bible called the principle of first usage. Basically how it is to be applied is that the first time a word (or subject) is presented in Scripture it should become the default setting from which all other usages are drawn from. When you apply that principle to worship, the starting place becomes Genesis 22:5. That's where Abraham speaks to his servants telling them that he and Isaac will, *"go over there; and we will worship and return to you."* (NASB) That's where worship is first mentioned in the Bible.

In Jewish history this scene is considered second in importance to the deliverance that took place at the crossing of the Red Sea. Its prominence in their religion (and in their congregational gatherings) is a touchstone of faith in action. It's an Ebenezer of sorts (a place of remembrance). But, here's the interesting and troubling thing about this story. It is a scene in which we are shown a father being commanded to effectively murder his only son as an act of sacrificial obedience. An act that Scripture tells us Abraham understood as being one of worship. There is just no way our temporal minds can embrace such a scenario as that without becoming totally confused and completely undone. It is simply beyond our understanding.

I'll include comments about this made by Eugene Peterson in his book *The Jesus Way*. His narrative on this event is insightful and well worth including here:

"The defining event in the way of Abraham takes place on Mount Moriah: The Binding of Isaac, the Akedah (the term the rabbis use for this story, after the Hebrew word for "binding"). Abraham binding Isaac, and offering him as a sacrifice on the altar that he has just built expressly for the purpose. This story has absorbed the imagination of the people of God and plunged generation after generation of us into facing and dealing with the fundamental mystery that is God: There is so much here that we cannot comprehend, so much that violates our pious sensibilities, so much that refuses to conform to our expectations. How can God command a murder? And not just murder in general but the murder of a beloved son? How can God go back on the miracle-promise fulfilled in the birth of Isaac? How can God, who our parents and pastors have taught us loves us from eternity, command this cold-blooded cruelty? How can God, who Jesus tells us has such a tender heart that he is moved even by the death of sparrows, command a father to kill his son, without so much as a hint of explanation?"

I would add, how in the process of carrying out such a difficult command, can Abraham call it worship?

From where we stand, on the other side of this biblical-historical story, how can we even begin to reach a place where our so called "contemporary worship" comes anywhere near embracing the depth of self-sacrifice and faithful obedience that we see in a scene such as this - and then call it worship? Yet, this story is where we find the first reference to worship taking place. It is where the biblical foundation of worship has been laid. It is here that we are provided a base on which to build. Regardless of how mysterious this may appear to us, it is nonetheless the starting point for how worship is to be approached and appropriated theologically. My personal perspective about all this is that we need to reboot our perception of what worship means, and then rebuild from there.

Note to readers: You might want to consider doing a Google search of "the binding" (Akedah) to gain a little more insight on the subject.

The Ins and Outs of Worship:

> *"What is here urged are secret habits of unceasing orientation of the depths of our being, ways of conducting our inward life so that we are perpetually bowed in worship."*
>
> ~T. Kelly

Outward expressions of worship (the visibly physical ones) should *always* be proceeded by inward engagement. Here's why:

In Genesis 22:1-5, we find Abraham preparing to offer up Isaac as a sacrifice of worship (see v.7). Before that sacrificial scene took place, Abraham had already settled inside himself that he would obey Jehovah's instruction/command. If he hadn't, then he would never have headed out toward the land of Moriah in the first place. His internal engagement was active *before* he began his faithful journey. The outward expression of obedience was based on his inward yielding to the voice of God - through an established and ongoing intimate relationship with his Lord. Based on what I shared in chapter #1, you should be able to see this scene as an act of consecration - for that's exactly what it is.

In Hebrew, the word *worship* in verse 7 means, to depress (i.e. to prostrate in homage to royalty or God); to bow (self); to crouch, fall down (flat); to humbly beseech; to show reverence, to make to stoop. Any visible attributes of Abraham's "worship" first manifested internally before flowing outward from an internal connection with God through obedient reverence.

The New Testament link up to the Old Testament principle found in Genesis 22:1-5 (worship through obedient service by faith) is seen in Hebrews 11:21. Out of all the stories the writer of Hebrews could have chosen to make a statement regarding worship, he used the passage from Genesis 47:31b as his go-to text.

> *"...then Israel bowed in worship at the head of the bed."*

There are two striking things expressed in that verse:

1. As was the case with Abraham in Genesis 22:1-5, the primary thing that was active with Jacob was his internal engagement – through intimate relationship with God. We see Jacob engaged in worship with little external evidence available to verify that worship is (in fact) taking place. But, according to Scripture, it certainly was.

2. The word *worship* in the Genesis 47 passage is translated the very same way in Hebrews 11:21. That builds a bridge which joins the foundational meaning of worship in the Old Testament directly to the meaning in the New Testament. That is huge!

In Revelation 4:9-10, we're shown a scene that's taking place in heaven, active in eternal time (past / present / future). In other words, the glimpse we are privileged to see was taking place, is taking place, and will always be taking place.

{Selah…pause and ponder}

Verse 10 tells us that the elders:

"…fall down before Him who sits on the throne, and will worship Him."

As was the case with Abraham, and Jacob, the external expressions of worship come forth from internal engagement – even in heaven. The word *worship* in v.10, carries the same meaning as it did for the writer of Hebrews in 11:21, Jacob in Genesis 47:31, and Abraham in Genesis 22:7. What the Bible conveys to us regarding worship, beginning with Abraham and ending with the elders around God's throne, is this:

Unless internal engagement first takes place in the life of a worshiper, any and all external expressions of worship could be considered as something less than scripturally viable or biblically based. Internal spiritual engagement establishes a channel through which outward expressions of worship can manifest. The best example that I know of in Scripture for identifying, understanding, and developing a biblical means for creating such a channel is presented in Paul's statement in Romans 12:1.

PONDERING(S)

> *"So here's what I want you to do, God helping you: Take your everyday, ordinary life - your sleeping, eating, going-to-work, and walking around life - and place it before God as an offering."*
>
> (The Message)

The life (lifestyle) that Paul is encouraging isn't one that is meant to take place only in our corporate / congregational gathering. Nor is it to be active in our so called "good works" for the Kingdom. The way that passage puts it, our very lives (24/7/365) are to be internally engaged prior to any other spiritual activity taking place. The NASB uses the phrase "service of worship" in Romans 12:1 regarding how we are to live out our lives as worshipers of the "One True God" (Deuteronomy 5:7). That wording was never intended to be interpreted as merely attending a "worship service." There is a huge difference between a worship service and the service of worship.

What's taking place inside, in our spirit-being, is (biblically speaking) where the action is. Thereafter, the outpouring (the manifestations) are to be external expressions of what's stirring inside.

> *"...for in Him we live, and move, and have our being."*
>
> ~Acts 17:28

There are three basic components of worship that I see as being biblically foundational. In the order of their priority they are:

1. A personal/intimate relationship to the subject of your worship (John 3:3)
2. Obedience to the will and ways of the object of your worship (John 5:30c)

3. A desire to grow and mature in your relationship with and obedience to the focus of your worship (John 15:5)

None of those three components have anything to do directly with what many believers currently consider to be worship. They do not mention emotions or feelings as such. Nor do that speak of any sort of "experience" (as in an event). In fact, they say nothing specifically about the outward evidences of worship at all. The contemporary aspects of worship that are visible in our corporate services should most certainly be involved (heart, soul, mind, body, and strength), but they are all outflows from relationship, obedience, and a desire to mature spiritually. The outward manifestations of worship are first birthed internally from within a person's spirit. If/When such engagement takes place, our beliefs are then released (by faith) as our external expressions of worship – as was the case with Abraham's offering of Isaac. Internal spiritual engagement produces (or should produce) external expansion of our expressions of worship. (See Psalm 35:10; Romans 12:1, The Message)

It's metaphor time: Think of worship as a stew being prepared in a large pot. All the aspects of our life are placed in the pot (Romans 12:1, The Message). We then place the cooking pot over a flame (which is the fire of the Holy Spirit). As the heat is turned up, the stew begins to boil, and steam begins to rise from out of the mixture. As it does, bubbles begin to work their way to the surface of the boiling stew and out into the atmosphere. The scent contained inside the pot is beginning to make its way to the outside of it – transforming an internal reality into an external expression. The bubbles are our praises arising from our lives of worship. As they ascend up and out of the pot the smell from the stew begins to fill the room with the fragrance that is contained in the pot. (Paraphrased from John Piper)

> *"May my prayer be counted as incense before You; the lifting up of my hands as the evening offering."*
>
> ~Psalm 141:2
> (NASB)

Before I share the story that's to follow, I want to give you a biblical perspective from which to read it. Try to consider it from a spiritual point of view rather than just a natural/temporal one. If it's read merely based on an earthly understanding, the supernatural implications could easily be overlooked altogether. Keep in mind that there are spiritual dynamics taking place in everything that happens in our lives and here on the earth. The eternal elements are really only discerned properly by those with (spiritual) eyes to see, and (spiritual) ears to hear.

> *"But a natural man does not accept the things of the Spirit of God, for they are foolishness to him; and he cannot understand them, they are spiritually appraised."*
>
> ~1 Corinthians 2:14
> (NASB)

Scripture tells us that the movement(s) of the Holy Spirit across the earth, and in the lives of people, isn't evident from a natural/earthly viewing. We're told that (like the wind), we can't see the Spirit. However, it is possible to see the evidence of the Spirit moving in the same way we see the evidence of the wind as it moves.

> *"You know well enough how the wind blows this way and that. You hear it rustling through the trees,*

WORSHIP

but you have no idea where it comes from or where it's headed next. That's the way it is with everyone 'born from above' by the wind of God, the Spirit of God."

~John 3:8
(The Message)

Now, put on your spiritual glasses and take a look at this:

Worship On The Wind
(A Personal Revelation)

"Blowing toward the south, then turning toward the north, the wind continues swirling along; and on its circular courses the wind returns."

~Ecclesiastes 1:6

In September of 2004, during my first sojourn to the continent of Africa, this happened: The story concerns an event that deeply impacted my life, my perceptions about living, and my future/destiny. In fact, the term "life-changing" is appropriate for what I have to share.

The story begins in late September of 2004 standing in the middle of nowhere in Kenya, Africa. I was returning with a short-term mission team from a region located in the very shadow of Mt. Kilimanjaro. We had spent 10 days or so building two church structures for the Maasai tribes, people who had converted to Christianity. After finishing and dedicating (consecrating) both buildings, we started our journey out of the "bush" toward a paved highway that would take us back to Nairobi. Driving along roads that really weren't roads at all, one of our Land Rovers broke down. Fortunately, our team guide had the know-how and the tools needed to make the necessary repairs. However, doing so was going to take a while. So, we all piled out of our vehicles and purposed to make the most of our time until things got sorted out.

{Waiting patiently for circumstances to change is a major part of the African lifestyle. It's in the DNA of those on the continent. If you go there, you will find that out for yourself.}

Here's what happened:

During our time together as a team we had learned that we weren't to walk too far away from the others when we were out in the "bush." Things can get dangerous in such an environment. So staying within eyesight of each other is pretty important. Our team leader had released us to roam the area near the vehicles, instructing us to stay close. We began to amble around in groups of two's and three's. A few of us went off on our own a brief distance away. I had walked away by myself to take care of nature's call behind a couple of scrub trees when something very unusual began to occur. As I turned to head back facing into the breeze that was rising up out of the valley opening up just below us, I heard what sounded like music.

More specifically it sounded like singing. To be exact it sounded like children singing. And to fine tune that even further, I heard children singing what seemed to me like worship. The "sound" was very brief – 2 or 3 seconds at the most. But I know worship when I hear it. It's a "deep calls to deep" thing (Psalm 42:7).

What I heard stunned me. How could this be happening? We were in "the middle of nowhere" so how could there be singing? Where would it come from? And, how could it be kids' voices?

As I continued to turn my face directly toward the

wind the sound disappeared. As soon as it was there, it was gone. I stopped in my tracks and began to try and figure out what was taking place. I turned my head ever so slightly to re-center myself, and when I did, the wind shifted and blew more directly into my ear again instead of straight into my face. When that happened the sound returned. This time it was as clear as a bell, but not very loud. Got the picture? So, now I'm getting excited because my brain (and my senses) are starting to catch up with my spirit. I turned my face directly back into the wind and the sound disappeared again. Now I was on to something that was beyond my immediate comprehension. As I turned my head away from the wind blowing at me directly, the air current blew into my ear again instead of into my face. Then what was happening hit me like a bolt of lightning. What I was hearing was on the wind – or in the wind. The sound was coming from somewhere as yet to be determined, and it was being carried by the wind itself. In fact, it couldn't be detected unless my ear was turned exactly the right way in order to catch the sound as it blew in my direction. In other words - without being positioned properly I couldn't hear the singing at all.

Saints, that'll preach!

I glanced back up the ridge to see if any of the others from the team knew what I was experiencing. Not a clue - they had heard nothing. They weren't positioned (tuned in) to it at all.

I was having a divine appointment and people within earshot of me had no idea!

{Selah…pause and ponder}

Once I realized what kind of "moment" I was in, I locked into the sound like a laser-tracking-beam. I began to

PONDERING(S)

move toward it. But, every time I turned directly into the wind I lost the singing. I could only stay on track by turning my head ever so slightly every few steps. That way the wind carried the sound into my ear and I could adjust my path of pursuit accordingly.

My heart was pounding and my soul was caught up in the dynamics of what was taking place. I had to know where the singing was coming from and who was creating it. So up toward the top of the ridge I ran yelling like a crazy man for the others to join me. But the angle I was moving in was taking me away from those on the team and the wind was carrying the sound of my voice (along with the sound of the singing) away from my comrades.

The only person near enough to really hear me was a sister from our worship choir back in our home church. As I motioned for her to meet me at the top of the ridge she began to head in that direction. She had no idea what was waiting up at the crest - and neither did I.

As Patti and I topped the rise of the ridge, we saw the valley opening up below us and beyond us toward a small mountain range in the distance. The valley wasn't very deep but it was fairly wide and long. As we looked down from the edge nearest us, we could see a dry river bed, which continued out and away from where we stood. At the base of the ridge just below us we saw something besides land and space. There was what appeared to be a sort of fort made from slender tree trunks which had been stripped clean of their bark. The fort was constructed in a rectangular shape and open to the sky. It had just four walls of wood with no ceiling. As we stood there trying to figure out what it was, suddenly everything locked into place in one profoundly amazing moment. The wind off the valley floor picked up and began to rise up the side of the ridge toward where we were positioned looking downward. And, what it carried up to us was now hitting us square in our faces. It was the sound of children singing at the top of their voices. It was such a precious and passionate sound. Such beauty and wonder in such a dry and barren place. This "no place" had become a high and holy place "in the middle of nowhere." I turned toward Patti who up until that moment had no idea of why I had called her to join me there. She hadn't heard a sound till it rose up on the wind and overwhelmed her. I looked at her with tears in my eyes (matched by her own) and I said, "Patti, it's a school and the kids are singing praise songs!" There under the open and expansive African sky the Holy Ghost fell big time, and my sister and I were overcome by the sound, tears, smiles and joy of it all.

In the very next instant one side of the "fort" opened up where a doorway was positioned and all the kids ran out of their classroom, made a turn away from us and moved out beyond and down into the dry riverbed laughing, jumping and having a grand time of it. I looked at Patti through more tears and I said, "It's recess." We both began to laugh out loud as we thanked God for His precious gift to us. As we stood there talking it all in the Holy Ghost spoke to me with a word of revelation. He said, "No place, is some place, to somebody." At that moment my global perspective exploded. My view of humanity, the nations, and God's ever-expanding Kingdom took on entirely new dimensions. My understanding of His Omnipresence had been blown totally off the charts. I was awestruck!

There's much more to this story than I've presented here. It continues to impact my life and ministry almost daily. But it's my understanding that pithy stories work best if they remain brief. So, I'll end with this:

PONDERING(S)

God's "otherness" is a very real thing to encounter. The eternal dynamics of His Kingdom - the ebb and flow - are constantly at work. We are "compassed about" (Psalm 32:7, KJV) by the sights and sounds of His Divine Presence in truly supernatural ways.

Allow the Spirit of the Lord to open up your senses, your soul and your very being to the glory and wonder of it all.

And may His Kingdom come (manifest) on earth as it is in heaven.

Let me mention one last thing to those of you who lead congregations in corporate worship on a regular basis. Please be encouraged by this *fact*! Worship, heart-felt, soul-engaged, pure, honest and undefiled worship is being released all over this earth every moment of every day (24/7/365). God has purposed and ordained it to be that way (Psalm 150:6; Luke 19:40). But, the thing is, we're not always standing in the right spot, at the right moment, with our heads turned just the right way to be able to hear it. Nonetheless, it is there. I can personally testify to the fact that there is worship on the wind coming from people in places that you'd never imagine.

> *"All of heaven's waiting*
> *All the earth expecting*
> *Sons, daughters, arise*
> *Singing songs of freedom*
> *Words of healing*
> *One voice, wind-blown worship"*
>
> ~From "Hallelujah"
> by Denise Graves

Enthroning God:

There is an interesting and overlooked aspect of worship that I want to address now. It has to do with one of the ways that God manifest His Presence among His people. The dynamics for it are found in Psalm 22:3 which says that, *"God is enthroned upon the praises of His people."* That verse is mentioned fairly often in congregations all over the world, but it is rarely taught on. As a result, many believers know the verse, but they don't know what it means. So, I'll try to unpack it for you.

Let's begin with the word *enthroned*. That term in the KJV is translated "inhabitest" (*yashab* in Hebrew) meaning to sit down (as a judge); to dwell, to remain; to settle; to marry; to establish; to make to keep house; to bring again into place; to remain, return to or tarry.

That word, its wide-ranging meanings, and what is represented by its usage in the Psalm 22:3 text speaks so profoundly to what is (or should be) taking place in the spiritual realm as we worship together. The definition(s) above provide us with a picture (or model) of what many of us say we are longing for when we come together as a congregation. We often say that we want God to "show up." You may have heard a pastor or a teacher state that the church needs a habitation from God, and not just a visitation. This verse is giving us a biblical explanation as to how that can happen. Let me add one more passage of Scripture to this mix in order to expand the context of what I'm saying. In 2 Chronicles 5:11-14, we're told this is what took place at the dedication of the Temple:

> *"The priests then left the Holy Place. All the priests there were consecrated, regardless of rank or assignment; and all the Levites who were musicians*

> *were there—Asaph, Heman, Jeduthun, and their families, dressed in their worship robes; the choir and orchestra assembled on the east side of the Altar and were joined by 120 priests blowing trumpets. The choir and trumpets made one voice of praise and thanks to GOD—orchestra and choir in perfect harmony singing and playing praise to GOD." Yes! God is good! His loyal love goes on forever! Then a billowing cloud filled The Temple of GOD. The priests couldn't even carry out their duties because of the cloud—the glory of GOD! — that filled The Temple of God."*

What we're looking at here is a worship service of monumental portion! Let's break it down:

- All the priests are there, in place, and *consecrated* for whatever takes place next.
- The Levites are there as well, also ready {consecrated} for any service that the Spirit might begin to orchestrate.
- Musicians and singers abound - and their praise offerings are loud and filled with passion. (Can you imagine what 120 trumpets would sound like in a Sunday service at your church?)
- The singers and musicians *"made one voice of praise and thanks to God."* In other words, they were not only prepared through consecration, they were also unified in their intentional sacrificial offerings. (See Psalm 133)
- Then, the Holy Spirit began to fill the atmosphere with His Presence – the weightiness of His glory (*kabod* in Hebrew).

The very thing that the people had hoped would happen in fact did. But, even though they had done their best to prepare for it, they still weren't ready for what took place. As a result, the service - for all practical purposes - was brought to an abrupt halt. The text says that no ministry was able to take place because the Lord took over. I wonder how many times comments are made in our churches about us being open to and willing for the Lord to take over our services and do whatever He wants to do?

Here's the thing about that: The end result of 2 Chronicles 5:14 was preceded by what took place in verses 11-13. Without the prep work transpiring first, why would we expect the same results to happen "in the house" when we gather for worship?

{Selah…pause and ponder}

Now, let's get back to unpacking Psalm 22:3.

Part of the definition for enthroning (inhabiting) is that of a judge sitting in a positon of authority. A better understanding of that might be to consider what a tribal chief does when those who live in the village gather before him whenever he sits outside his hut in order to provide counsel and direction to the community-at-large. In other words, he takes his seat of authority in order to address the details of how the people are to conduct themselves with one another, live their lives, raise their families, and interact with other tribes within the region. Isn't that something we hope that the Lord will do for and with us?

> *"The steps of a good man are established by the Lord."*
>
> ~Psalm 37:23a
> (NASB)

PONDERING(S)

> *"Establish my footsteps in Your word, and do not let any iniquity have dominion over me."*
> ~Psalm 119:133
> (NASB)

Another aspect of this enthroning is to marry and set up housekeeping. (The Hebrew language is very visual in its usage). The implication is that in doing so, the intension is to reside in one place – dwell – where an inviting and accommodating space has been set up, like, say, a throne. That dear reader, is what many of us say we want God to do, dwell among us. Not just come and visit, rather, come and abide.

> *"Holy Spirit, You are welcome here*
> *Come flood this place and fill the atmosphere*
> *Your glory God, is what our hearts long for*
> *To be overwhelmed by Your Presence, Lord"*
> ~Bryan and Katie Torwalt

That currently popular lyric speaks directly to what God wants to do when He comes among us. Change the atmosphere, give direction to our lives (personally and corporately), counsel us on how to maintain our communities. In essence, rule over and among us as our Sovereign! Do you see what I'm saying?

> *"Say what you hear, so that you can see what you say."*
> ~Bishop Joseph Garlington

Another word for *inhabites*t in Scripture is the word *sit* which is often translated as *yashab* in the Hebrew language. There is one passage in particular that gives us an astounding picture of what it means when someone is sitting in the exalted position of *yashab*. It is found in Job

29 beginning in verse 7 where Job is speaking of himself. He says, *"When I went out to the gate of the city, when I took my seat in the square…"* The seat he's mentioning is the place where he is sitting in yashab. Everything that is mentioned from there till the end of the chapter, describes what took place when he was seated there, and how others were impacted by him doing so. Please take the time to read what it says. As you do, consider this: The description presented there in regards to Job, is exactly the role that God wants to have among His people when we are gathered, offering praises in worship, upon which He is then enthroned (seated / yashabed). The very thought of how this biblical concept could impact our church services just blows me away!

The next word in Psalm 22:3 to consider is the word *praises*. Note please that it is not singular in its usage, it's plural. It is expressed in regards to a group of people in song, not to an individual singing alone.

> *"Where two are three have gathered together in My name, I am there in their midst."*
>
> ~Matthew 18:20
> (NASB)

In the Hebrew it is *tehillah*, meaning to laud or offer laudation. It has to do with singing. But not singing singularly. It's not used here as personal singing. It's referring to congregational singing. It takes place in corporate worship. Think of it as a "one voice" expression much like the dynamic expressed in the 2 Chronicles 5 passage I already mentioned. It is not a passive word. Nor is it non-active, it's pro-active. It is filled with passion, zeal, and gusto. It comes from the base word *halah*, which means to shine; to make a show; to boast; to act clamorously foolish; to rave and celebrate; to act foolish. I'm not making this stuff up. Don't shout me down!

> *"No chorus is too loud, no orchestra too large, no Psalm too lofty for the lauding of the Lord of Hosts."*
>
> (C. Spurgeon)

Between the words *enthroned* and *praises*, there is one more little word we need to consider. It's the word *on*. The verse says that God is enthroned (*on*) the praises of His people. What the word *on* tells us is that the throne itself is built out of (fashioned from) our praises. Yep, that's what it says. You see, when we gather together with the intentional purpose of enthroning God, we become throne builders. What we create with our sacrificial offerings of praise is somehow supernaturally transformed into the very seat of authority that God wants to come and occupy in the midst of us (Psalm 22:22-25; Psalm 116:19). Once seated there, all the things that He desires to impart to us as His people then begin to flow out of the Spirit directly into our lives (both personally and corporately). That is astounding. The possibilities are breathtaking to imagine.

> *"On the whole, I do not find Christians, outside of the catacombs, sufficiently sensible of conditions. Does anyone have the foggiest idea what sort of power we so blithely invoke? Or, as I suspect, does no one believe a word of it? The churches are children playing on the floor with their chemistry sets, mixing up a batch of TNT to kill a Sunday morning. It is madness to wear ladies' straw hats and velvet hats to church; we should all be wearing crash helmets. Ushers should issue life preservers and signal flares; they should lash us to our pews.*

WORSHIP

> *For the sleeping god may wake someday and take offense, or the waking god may draw us out to where we can never return."*
>
> ~Annie Dillard

Let's work all this a little more.

If our praises are the substance from which the throne of praise is built, it would then follow that the amount of praise we bring with us "in the house" determines the size of the throne itself. Once construction is completed, the purpose of building it can then take place - which is to enthrone God. When He comes to sit on the throne we've built for Him, He will occupy it (or fill it) with His Divine Presence. Now, hold that thought as I share with you a story (a revelation) which applies specifically to what I'm sharing.

Years ago, I read a book by Tommy Tenney entitled, *God's Favorite House*. In it there is a chapter called "Building A Mercy Seat." Although the focus of that chapter isn't about throne building as such, the story draws a parallel that has stuck with me till today. I've shared it in many teaching sessions and in many nations. Here it is:

Tenney once had a man in his church that was very large. In fact, he was extremely overweight. During the time he was in fellowship there, he grew less and less sociable in terms of his interaction with others at the church. One day, Tenney took him aside and asked him why he had withdrawn from the relationships he'd been active in. The gentleman said that he had to stop going to people's homes when he was invited because when he got there he couldn't find any place to sit down; there were no pieces of furniture large enough or solid enough to hold his weight. That made him sad, and it made those he had gone to visit uncomfortable - creating an awkward situation for everybody there. As a result, he just stopped going when he was invited.

That story applies what I've been sharing in this matter: God's Presence, His glory (*kabod* – see 2 Chronicles 5:14) is expansive and weighty. When He's wanting to manifest, His intention is to fill up the places where He is. So, the more room there is for Him to "show up," the more of Him will (in fact) show up.

{Little throne, little Presence, big throne, big Presence}

One of the most impactful books in my library addressing the subject of praise is entitled, *The Hallelujah Factor*, written by Jack Taylor. In the chapter "The Preview of Praise" there is a sub-section which he calls, "Praise Is Where God Lives." In it, Taylor says this (in part):

> *"While God is everywhere, He is not everywhere manifested. He is at home in praise and, being at home, He manifests Himself best as God! When you or I choose to make God at home through praise, we invite Him to act "at home." When God is "at home" in praise He does what He wants to do."*

Can I get an *Amen*?

I have one more word picture for you to help you to see what I'm saying in regards to how collective-corporate-praise-offerings can serve to create an atmosphere in which God will move in power as He chooses. It's found in another of my "treasures old and new" (Matthew 13:52). The copyright is 1975. I've worn it out having read it over and over for decades. The little book is entitled, *Destined for*

The Throne, by Paul E. Billheimer. It is still in print, and for a very good reason. In it, Billheimer says this about the size and impact of our corporate praise.

> *"To be most effective, then, praise must be massive, continuous, a fixed habit, a full-time occupation, a diligently pursued vocation, a total way of life. This principle is emphasized in Psalm 57:7: "My heart is fixed, O God, my heart is fixed; I will sing and give praise." This suggests a premediated and predetermined habit of praise. This kind of praise depends on something more than temporary euphoria. It is perpetual, purposeful, and aggressive. Praise is the spark plug of faith. It is the one thing needed to get faith airborne, enabling it to soar above deadly doubt. Praise is the detergent which purifies faith and purges doubt from the heart. The secret of answered prayer is faith without doubt (Mark 11:23). And the secret of faith without doubt is praise – continuous, massive, triumphant praise, praise that is a way of life."*

Praise, our congregational praises, provide us with the materials to build a throne for our Sovereign to sit on as He dwells among, us imparting all the things we need to live as citizens of heaven, ministers of reconciliation, and ambassadors for Christ (see 2 Corinthians 5:18-21).

PONDERING(S)

THE BEST SEAT IN THE HOUSE
(Psalm 22:3)

Make room, make way
We've come into His house to bless Him today
Make some noise, lift up a shout,
Do what you have to do to get your worship out
(Our God deserves), the best seat in the house

Lord, come and take Your rightful place
You are due the highest honor,
So we're building You a throne of praise
The heavens cannot contain You,
Of that there is no doubt
We welcome Your Holy Presence
(You deserve), the best seat in the house

Take a stand, make a choice,
Open up the heavens with the sound of your voice
State it clear, say it plain,
Do what you've got to do to declare Him as King
(Our God deserves), the best seat in the house

Lord, come and take Your rightful place
You are due the highest honor,
So we're building You a throne of praise
The heavens cannot contain You,
Of that there is no doubt
We welcome Your Holy Presence
(You deserve), the best seat in the house

(W. Berry, See and Say Songs, BMI)

CHAPTER 3
Pondering Presence

"But as for me, the nearness of God is my good."
~Psalm 73:28a

"The times for the depths of the silences of the heart seem so few. And in guilty regret we must postpone till next week that deeper life of unshaken composure in the Holy Presence."

~T. Kelly

Where is God not? That's a question worth pondering for sure.

In classic theology, the concept of "Divine Simplicity" addressed three characteristics of God's being: Omnipresence (His every-where-ness), Omnipotence (His all-powerful-ness), and Omniscience (His all-knowing-ness). Paul says, God is 'all in all' (1 Corinthians 15:28), with no division between person and attributes. In this chapter I'll be focusing in on the aspect of God's Omnipresence. I haven't acquired the ability to plumb the depths of what that subject means, not yet, if ever. But I do have a perspective to offer based on my (wait for it) ponderings.

God's Presence, and how we perceive it, impacts both topics I've addressed thus far. I've considered consecration and worship in the previous two chapters. Each of those subjects are linked together with the idea of establishing a relationship with the one we are consecrated to serve, and who or what we worship. Presence has a direct bearing on how intimate such a relational fellowship is formed - how personal it is.

> *"In the early stages we do not watch with Jesus, we watch for Him."*
>
> ~O. Chambers

An Axiom
Knowledge is Information
Understanding is Interpretation
Wisdom is Application

Back to The Garden:

> *"God, who is everywhere, never leaves us. Yet He seems sometimes to be present, sometimes to be absent. If we do not know Him well, we do not realize that He may be more present to us when He is absent than when He is present."*
>
> ~Thomas Merton

In order to deal with the concept of establishing an intimate relationship with the Sovereign God of the universe, the beginning of the very first such relationship would be the place to start. So, I'll begin there, where humankind is introduced to the Creator. In The Garden.

Genesis 1:2 tells us that the earth was *"formless and void."* There were no local residents. From there, the act(s) of creation began to manifest. Progressively thereafter, the account of Adam being formed from the dust, and Eve being fashioned from his rib, unfolds. At that stage in the history of humanity, there was no such thing as theology. It wasn't necessary because there were no people on the planet to be schooled in or concerned about the nature and the ways of God. Without anyone being available to interact with their Maker, a relationship would have been impossible. For a spiritually supernatural relationship to become active there had to be at least two sides to it - between God and man.

{There can be no intimacy without someone to be intimate with.}

The introduction of God's Presence to humankind began to unfold during this early phase of His relational development with the first two human creations (Genesis 2). First, He established communication through some spoken manner with Adam (Genesis 2:16). Thereafter, God fashioned Eve, and in doing so He expanded the circle of relational intimacy. Let's re-examine this story with the intention of looking for Presence to appear:

> They (Adam and Eve) *"heard the sound of the Lord God walking in the garden in the cool of the day, and the man and his wife hid themselves from the Presence of the Lord God."*
> ~Genesis 3:8

There are two major things taking place in that verse that provide us with an understanding in regards to the development of the theology of omnipresence.

First, by stating that Adam and Eve heard the sound of the Lord walking among them, the text is implying /

indicating that they only knew that God was around when they perceived some sort of manifestation of Him.

{For many believers, that is still an issue today.}

In other words, when they weren't aware of Him being *there*, they assumed that he wasn't. That's because they had no comprehension of Him being everywhere all the time. Why? Because God had not educated (taught/discipled) them in the concept of omnipresence. No such theology existed. In other words, they had no cognitive context for His ever-present-ness at that stage of their relationship with Him. They weren't aware He was there unless He made His Presence known to them in some way.

Next, the reality of this is confirmed in the same verse when we're told that Adam and Eve *"hid themselves from His Presence."* You see, they thought that they in fact could hide from Him because they didn't realize that there was no place that He was not already present. So, hiding from Him seemed to not only be possible to them, it also seemed logical for them to do so, due to their fear of being exposed to Jehovah face to face because of their original sin. We know that because of what we're told in verse 10. Adam states, *"I heard the sound of You in the garden, and I was afraid."* He also says that he knew that he (and Eve) were naked (exposed) before God. At that very moment sin had already entered in their relationship with God, and the intimate relationship that they had with His Presence up to that point was breaking down even as the conversation was taking place. A lamentably heartbreaking event!

> *"Adam, with Eve, is a "stand-in" for every human. They were not satisfied to be dependent on God (naked & unashamed); they wanted to be more than human. Rejecting their limitations, they*

> *lost their unashamed condition and became less than human. The origin of all sin (original sin) is the desire to be other than who you are. When they covered themselves with fig leaves, they were hiding from God and one another. Shame's goal realized: ruptured relationships."*
>
> ~Fount Shults

I personally believe that the issue of being able to acknowledge and maintain awareness of God's ongoing omnipresence began as this scene was unfolding. I further believe that the relational break which took place in this story was (and is) at the very heart of God's plan of salvation in Christ Jesus' redemptive work through His birth, death, burial and resurrection. I use as my scriptural rationale for such a statement, this one verse:

> *"For it was fitting for Him for whom are all things, and through whom are all things, in bringing many sons to glory, to perfect the author of their salvation through suffering."*
>
> ~Hebrews 2:10

That verse sums up how I see the salvific plan unfolding after the relational division took place in Genesis 3. That text tells us how God intended to repair the breach - by perfecting the Author of our salvation. It also tells us why He did so – in order to bring many sons (and daughters) into glory. You see, God has always wanted humankind to be in intimate relationship with Him. How do I know that? Because that's what Scripture tells me was the incentive for creating man in the first place:

> *"Then God said, "Let Us make man in Our image, according to Our likeness."*
>
> ~Genesis 1:26

PONDERING(S)

The Holy Trinity is the Divine and eternal example of complete and total unity in relationship – the 3 in One. As such, the desire for such relationship(s) to be established between the Trinity and humankind has always been set deeply within the heart of the Father, Son, and Holy Ghost.

{Selah…pause and ponder}

Moving forward from the narrative of The Garden, we come to another passage of Scripture addressing an incomplete theological understanding of omnipresence. In Exodus 33:13-17, we're told that Moses addresses the Lord with a very specific request in regards to His Presence. I consider the prayer in this passage to be one of the most (if not the most) important prayers in the entire Old Testament. The *why* of it has a direct effect on how the process of gaining insight and understanding takes place biblically regarding God's Presence abiding in and moving through us.

Let's consider the story together:

Moses' Prayer for Presence:

> *"I must first have the sense of God's possession of me before I can have the sense of His Presence with me."*
>
> ~Watchman Nee

For context, Moses is about to lead the wilderness children from where they are to where they aren't yet – a sojourning. That process is embedded in the spiritual DNA of those who live upon the earth as "strangers and pilgrims" (Hebrews 11:13). The call upon the citizens of heaven is "from strength to strength" (Psalm 84:5-7) leaving a deposit of righteousness, peace, and joy wherever they go (Romans 14:7), shinning as light in a dark land (Ephesians 5:8). The call upon God's children is always upward "from glory to glory" (2 Corinthians 3:18) in their journey toward heaven and home.

PONDERING(S)

CORRIDOR OF LIGHT

If I'm in a bad circumstance,
with very few choices
Caught up in the chaos,
hearing very strange voices
There's a path that I can take,
it's the way for me to go
Down the corridor of light,
there's a hand that I can hold

CHORUS:
When I'm liftin' up Jesus, when I'm liftin' up Jesus
When I'm liftin' up Jesus, I'm takin' demons down

Even at the end of the age,
there's a promise I can claim
I can dignify the trial,
when I call upon on His name
Then in the middle of the warfare,
or at the end of my rope
I see a corridor of light,
where there's a glimmer left of hope

REPEAT CHORUS:

We're movin' from glory to glory,
from strength to strength
From one level to another,
we're all done with unbelief
With our eyes toward Zion,
God's Holy hill
We'll see the corridor of light,
that shines and always will

REPEAT CHORUS:

(W. Berry, See and Say Songs, BMI)

PRESENCE

In pursuit of Kingdom destiny there is a fundamental protocol to be followed. It is to live in obedience to upholding the purposes of God in our lives. Yielding ourselves to those purposes points us directly towards our destiny. In other words, we fulfill our destiny when we live in obedient service to the purposes of God in our lives. The supporting factor which equips us to give ourselves over to God's Sovereign will is the provision of His grace.

If we define grace as being simply unmerited Divine favor, then we have made it far too small in our understanding. For it is so much more than that. Here's the definition that I use for you to take to heart:

> *Grace is the empowering Presence of God, enabling me to be who He created me to be, so that I can do what He's called me to do.*

I got that definition from either Bishop Joseph Garlington, or Pastor James Ryle. They both deserve credit for having shared it.

> *"After centuries of handling and mishandling, most religious words have become so shopworn nobody's much interested anymore. Not so with grace, for some reason. Mysteriously, even derivatives like gracious and graceful still have some of the bloom left. Grace is something you can never get but can only be given. There's no way to earn it or deserve it or bring it about any more than you can deserve the taste of raspberries and cream or earn good looks or bring about your own birth. A good sleep is grace and so are good dreams. Most tears are grace. The smell of rain is grace. Somebody loving you is grace. Loving somebody is grace. Have you ever tried to love somebody?*

PONDERING(S)

"A crucial eccentricity of the Christian faith is the assertion that people are saved by grace. There's nothing you have to do. There's nothing you have to do. There's nothing you have to do. The grace of God means something like:

"Here is your life. You might never have been, but you are, because the party wouldn't have been complete without you. Here is the world. Beautiful and terrible things will happen. Don't be afraid. I am with you. Nothing can ever separate us. It's for you I created the universe. I love you." There's only one catch. Like any other gift, the gift of grace can be yours only if you'll reach out and take it. Maybe being able to reach out and take it is a gift too."

~Frederick Buechner

PRESENCE

CLOSER TO THE CLOUD

*If Your Spirit doesn't go before me,
I'm not movin', I'm stayin' here
If Your fire doesn't light my path,
then this is where I'll be
Until I know You've made a way,
I'll keep resting, and waiting, Lord
Listening till I hear You say,
'Child, it's time'*

*CHORUS:
Draw me closer to the cloud, when it starts moving
Closer to the heart of what You're doing
Closer to the Kingdom I'm pursuing
Draw me closer to the cloud*

*If the glory of Your Holy Hand isn't on me,
then I'm undone
How else can I fulfill Your plan,
without Your Holy touch
No one else would understand,
it's Your Presence that changes me
So Father, this is where I'll stand
until it's time*

REPEAT CHORUS:

(W. Berry, See and Say Songs, BMI)

PONDERING(S)

In that context, Moses prays an impassioned prayer that is to impact all those who come after him by faith.

> *"Now therefore, I pray You, if I have found favor in Your sight, let me know Your ways that I may know You, so that I may find favor in Your sight. Consider too, that this nation is Your people." And He said, "My Presence shall go with you, and I will give you rest." Then he said to Him, "If Your Presence does not go with us, do not lead us up from here. For how then can it be known that I have found favor in Your sight, I and Your people? Is it not by Your going with us, so that we, I and Your people, may be distinguished from all the other people who are upon the face of the earth?" The LORD said to Moses, "I will also do this thing of which you have spoken; for you have found favor in My sight and I have known you by name."*
>
> ~Exodus 33:13-17
> (NASB)

When this passage is unpacked, we begin to see a magnificent promise unfolding not only to provide an answer for Moses on behalf of himself and those he is leading. But, also to all those who will come after him who have a desire for an intimate relationship with their Lord. The outworking of this story and this prayer is grand, glorious, and profound in its implications.

I'll call your attention to two things in particular contained in the powerful prayer:

1. Moses prays for himself and for the people he's responsible for (Exodus 33:16). That is a model of how spiritual leadership should serve God by serving His people. It is also a model

of how important the ministry of intercession is when beseeching the Lord for favor, guidance, protection, and provision (see Daniel 9 for a display of "identificational repentance" through intercession).
2. The main subject of the prayer is Presence and its pending influence upon those who don't know God. In that sense, and from that perspective it is a prayer of evangelism which serves as a forerunner of the so called "Great Commission" (Matthew 28:19-20), and the charge and sending of Acts 1:8. I'll have more to say about that in the next chapter.

The fundamental motivation for Moses' prayer (i.e. the subject of it) is Jehovah's abiding Presence and the impact it can have on those who have no knowledge of Him - no relationship with Him. As Moses prays he doesn't ask for signs and wonders, miracles, blessing, riches, power, favor, popularity, church growth, a personal or corporate dynasty, etc. His prayer is singular in its intention and profound in its focused request. That is apparent when he says,

"For how then can it be known that I have found favor in Your sight, I and Your people? Is it not by Your going with us, so that we, I and Your people, may be distinguished from all the other people who are upon the face of the earth?"

The phrase *"for how then can it be known"* is in reference to the people that are to be encountered as they move out beyond where they are at the time the prayer is being offered up. Since Moses is leading the people into territory where they've never been, there is the likelihood that they will interact with people(s) that haven't heard of, believed in, or had the opportunity to serve the One True God (see Deuteronomy 5:7). Today, those people are found all over the world. They occupy all the nations of the earth, and the gift of (and the ministry of) reconciliation is available to *everyone* who will receive it (2 Corinthians 5:18-19). The original expression of the job description for every "born again" believer was drafted the very moment that Moses uttered that phrase. We are ambassadors of Christ because of Moses' heartfelt intercession for the lost. For that we should be eternally grateful, and humbled in contrition for his concern to see God's Kingdom advanced and increased on this terrestrial ball.

> *"Therefore, we are ambassadors for Christ, as though God were making an appeal through us; we beg you on behalf of Christ, be reconciled to God. He made Him who knew no sin to be sin on our behalf, so that we might become the righteousness of God in Him."*
>
> ~2 Corinthians 5:20, 21
> (NASB)

There's another very detailed (and revealing) word in the closing sentence of this prayer. That word is *distinguished* (NASB). In the KJV it's translated as *separated*, meaning to distinguish; to put a difference, show as marvelous, to set apart, to make wonderful. Dear reader, that is the very thing that Peter says God's people are to be on earth under the New Testament covenant:

> *"But you are a chosen race, a royal priesthood, a holy nation, a people for God's own possession, so*

> *that you may proclaim the excellencies of Him who has called you out of darkness into His marvelous light…"*
>
> ~1 Peter 1:9
> (NASB)

The genesis of Christian identity is located in Moses' prophetic prayer on behalf of ALL of the children of God, chosen and elected to represent the Kingdom on earth, as it is in heaven (Matthew 6:9-13).

{I am undone! I simply must stop here, bow down on my knees before my Sovereign, and offer up myself again in worship and praise, with adoration, and exaltation to Him for all those who have come before me and made a way for me to be known by and accepted in the Beloved. ~Ephesians 1:6}

> *"From the moment we claim the truth of being in the Beloved, we are faced with the call to become who we are. Becoming the Beloved is the great spiritual journey we have to make."*
>
> ~Henri Nouwen

A Pathway to Presence:

> *"How blessed is the man whose strength is in You, in whose heart are the highway(s) to Zion!"*
>
> ~Psalm 84:5
> (NASB)

I've uncovered (or discovered) what I believe is a biblical protocol for how Presence progressed from Moses' prayer all the way to up Pentecost and beyond.

PONDERING(S)

**Presence precedes Power
Power prompts Witness
Witness proclaims Testimony
Testimony produces Kingdom Expansion**
~Exodus 33, Matthew 28, Acts 1:8

Here's the outworking of that protocol:

Presence precedes Power:

Moses prays specifically for Presence to go with the wilderness wanderers. God agrees that He will answer that prayer in the affirmative: The Power, meant to transform them in such a way as to be known (distinguished) as a people set apart, is what validates God's answer to Moses' request. The Power comes along with the Presence, but it comes *after* the Presence – not before. It isn't given for the sake of "signs and wonders" as such. It is imparted in order to establish a people set part for the sake of the Kingdom calling upon their lives, both personally and corporately.

CROWN OF GLORY

For Zion's sake I will not keep silent
For Jerusalem's sake I will not be still
Until salvation burns eternal
And righteousness shines like a light on a hill

CHORUS:
Then you will be a crown of glory
To reign with Him in majesty
You will be a crown of glory
A holy people, the redeemed
(Known by a new name,
known by a brand new name)

Upon the walls, there are watchmen standing
All day and all night, they will remain
Reminding the Lord, of His blessed promise
And in the might of His strength they shall remain

REPEAT CHORUS:

No longer forsaken, no longer barren
A delight to the Lord, we shall be married to Him
Go through the gates, the gates of Zion
Build up the "highway of holiness"
Take out the stones and lift up the banners
For surely our salvation's come at last

REPEAT CHORUS:
    (W. Berry & Brian Darnel, See and Say Songs, BMI)

Power prompts Witness:

As the people move out into other regions and among other people groups that have no knowledge or understanding of Jehovah, the people themselves become living witnesses based on their personal and corporate relationships with their Lord. That witness doesn't require anything of them except to show up carrying the Presence with them in their lives. The Power that's been imparted to them through Presence has created a spiritual reality in their very being which emanates through them, thereby changing both the atmosphere and the environment anywhere and everywhere they go.

Witness proclaims Testimony:

From their lives as living witnesses, testimony is birthed. Who they have become as witnesses (empowered by the indwelling Presence of God) releases them to describe what has taken place in their midst as children of the Most High (Psalm 104). What they say has a ring of authenticity to it because it is validated by their living witness, and the Power of God's Divine Presence.

Testimony produces Kingdom Expansion:

What they say, by faith, is the proclamation of the gospel of the Kingdom, in seed form carried all the way from when the "Promised Land" was entered and beyond. Those testimonies became the basis for what we now call evangelism, which in turn added converts from among those who would come to believe the testimonies they heard. The result of that was/is souls won for Christ, which produces Kingdom expansion.

That protocol provided the foundation on which the so called "Great Commission" is built. The charge that Jesus gave to his 12 disciples relates directly to the process that grew out of God's answer to Moses' prayer:

> *"And Jesus came up and spoke to them, saying, "All authority has been given to Me in heaven and on earth. Go therefore and make disciples of all the nations, baptizing them in the name of the Father, and the Son, and the Holy Spirit, teaching them to observe all that I commanded you; and lo, I am with you always, even to the end of the age."*
> ~Matthew 28:18-20 (NASB)

Jesus (the Son) speaking with the authority given Him by God (the Father) places a charge upon those *disciples (I'll say more about discipleship in the following chapter) who are with Him (in His Presence). The charge is to go forth (as did Moses and those he was leading) into the nations (regions where the knowledge and acceptance of God was not prevalent). While there - as living witnesses - they were to give testimony to who God was and who He is in them (by teaching/discipling the nations). Then Christ closes out His directive by assuring them that He will be with them (that His Presence will go where they are being sent).

Note, please, that the last statement is really a prerequisite to the coming of the Holy Ghost at Pentecost.

From there, the scriptural narrative takes us to Acts 1:8. It's there that the continued unfolding of Moses' answered prayer, and the charge from Jesus to His 12 disciples, becomes the launching platform for all those who have come into the Kingdom of God by being "born again" into a "new and living way" (Hebrews 10:20).

> *"But you will receive power when the Holy Spirit has come upon you; and you shall be My witnesses both in Jerusalem, and in all Judea and Samaria, and even to the remotest part of the earth."*
>
> ~Acts 1:8
> (NASB)

The promise of Pentecost is bound together with the earnest prayer that Moses offered up so many centuries ago. Watch this…

You shall receive Power (after) the Holy Spirit comes (which is the manifestation of God's Holy Presence). It (the Power) doesn't come before the Presence, it comes after. Then the 12 disciples become Witnesses. They don't go out and witness. No, they become Witnesses. The text says, "You shall be MY witnesses." Thereafter, they were to be empowered by the indwelling Presence of the Holy Ghost. That empowerment (as living witnesses) was what was to give them the ability to carry out the very thing that Jesus charged them to do in the so called "Great Commission." The phrase, *"even to the remotest part of the earth"* is precisely what they were told to go and do in Matthew 28:19, *"go and make disciples of all the nations."* I see that as pretty amazing stuff right there. And you, how do you see it? What's the Spirit showing you, I wonder?

Up to this point in this chapter I've been laying the groundwork for what's to follow. The progression from here in regards to God's omnipresence has been and still is a major point of pondering for me over the last 30+ years. Stay with me and I'll show you some more of what I've been learning these last 2 ½ decades.

PRESENCE

We know that Jehovah answered Moses' prayer because Scripture tells us that He did.

> *"The LORD said to Moses, "I will also do this thing of which you have spoken; for you have found favor in My sight and I have known you by name."*
> ~Exodus 33:17

At some point in that process of our spiritual history, the theology of Presence (omnipresence) began to be revealed. I'm not certain exactly when and where it took place. I'm still working on sorting that all out. But I know that it did. Here's how I know:

> *"Where can I go from Your Spirit? Or where can I flee from Your Presence? If I ascend to heaven, You are there; if I make my bed in Sheol, behold, You are there. If I take the wings of the dawn, if I dwell in the remotest part of the sea, even there Your hand will lead me, and Your right hand will lay hold of me. If I say, "Surely the darkness will overwhelm me, and the light around me will be night," Even the darkness is not dark to You, and the night is as bright as the day.*
> *Darkness and light are alike to You."*
> ~Psalm 139:7-12

The Psalmist has an awareness of God's ever-everywhere-Presence that is undeniable! The prophetic insights contained in this passage are directly linked to Moses' prayer for God's Presence to abide with His people. The longing that Moses expressed has been (over time) fulfilled as is apparent by what David is saying through his statement.

PONDERING(S)

Another aspect of how omnipresence is at work everywhere and all the time is declared in David's expression. He states:

> *"Surely the darkness will overwhelm me, and the light around me will be night," "Even the darkness is not dark to You, and the night is as bright as the day. Darkness and light are alike to You."*
>
> ~Psalm 139:12

That is a statement that we have either disregarded, overlooked, or perhaps simply chosen to ignore in our contemporary approach to Presence.

My opening question at the beginning of this chapter was, "Where is God not?" David addresses that question in this passage as he gives his answer in verse 7 by saying there is no place he can go that God isn't. He then expands that revelation by adding a specific statement dealing with a subject that we tend to do all we can to avoid. He says:

> *"Even darkness is not dark to You, and the night is as bright as the day. Darkness and light are alike to You."*

There is likely nowhere else in Scripture where such a stunningly overwhelming declaration of God's sovereignty is mentioned.

What an expansive and all-inclusive pronouncement!

The perspective continues to widen out from there when the prophet Isaiah hits it with even more light as he unfolds this picture of Presence:

> *"I will give you the treasures of darkness and hidden wealth of secret places, so that you may know that it is I, The LORD, the God of Israel, who calls you by your name."*
>
> ~Isaiah 45:3

David says that darkness and light are the same to God. Isaiah says, speaking prophetically for Jehovah, that there are treasures of darkness (or treasures hidden in darkness) that the Lord will give those who find themselves in such places. He further states the reason that God will do that is so that those who find themselves in such situations will know that the call of God is still resounding and resident there - because there is no place where He isn't present. At least that's how the passage reads to me.

Here's part of what I see in these two expositions: It appears to me that God is saying that there are things of value (treasures and hidden wealth) in places of darkness. He is also implying that those who find themselves in such places can be given those things, which they can then in turn carry with them when they come out. Yep, that's what I see. If I look further, into the New Testament, I also see links (or hear echoes) of this same dynamic at work in the comments of James 1:2-3:

> *"Consider it all joy, my brethren, when you encounter various trials, knowing that the testing of your faith produces endurance. And let endurance have its perfect result, so that you may be perfect and complete, lacking in nothing."*
>
> ~James 1:2-4
> (NASB)

That's also reinforced in verse 17 stating that:

> *"Every good thing given and every perfect gift is from above, coming down from the Father of lights, with whom there is no variation or shifting shadow."*
>
> ~James 1:17
> (NASB)

PONDERING(S)

We have become conditioned to believe that we are to do everything we can to remove ourselves from darkness. Rebuke it, run from it, disavow it, basically take no part in it. That is, in some cases, the correct thing for us to do. But not always. If that is the only response we have to darkness, then what do we do with the passages from Psalm 139, Isaiah 45, and James 1:2,3 and 17? Could we perhaps be missing out on things that God intends for us to have a share in which are beneficial to our lives - and the lives of those we come in contact with – by doing whatever we can to avoid places of difficulty, and struggle found in dark places?

{Selah... pause and ponder}

> *"Sometimes the best map cannot give you*
> *You can't see what's 'round the bend*
> *Sometimes the road leads through dark places*
> *Sometimes the darkness is your friend"*
>
> ~Bruce Cockburn

Work this through with me:

Jesus is the light of the world (John 1:1-5) and we are children of light (Ephesians 5:8). As sharers of the light of the Lord, Scripture says we are to expose the deeds of darkness (Ephesians 5:11). It doesn't say we are to run from them. Light shines in dark places merely by showing up. It doesn't necessarily have to do anything. Nothing is required of it except that it shines in any place where darkness exist. If light happens to be placed where darkness is, then to the degree of brightness the light contains, darkness is dispelled proportionally.

I'm not saying that we as "children of light" are to go into dark places of our own accord. Actions like that can get us into lots of trouble. We should only enter such places if circumstances place us there allowed by (and sometimes orchestrated) by the hand of the Lord, or by the leadings and promptings of the Spirit. However, when we find ourselves in such places of darkness, perhaps before we try to somehow get ourselves out of them, we might first consider extending the light we carry – the light we are – into them. God only knows how such places might be changed by doing so. And, there's no way of knowing beforehand what kind of treasures and hidden wealth we might take out of them when we leave them.

> *"You are the light of the world. A city set on a hill cannot be hidden; nor does anyone light a lamp and put it under a basket, but on the lampstand, and it gives light to all who are in the house. Let your light shine before men in such a way that they may see your good works, and glorify your Father who is in heaven."*
>
> ~Matthew 5:14-16 (NASB)

> *"Nothing worth having comes without some kind of fight; You've got to kick at the darkness till it bleeds daylight."*
>
> ~Bruce Cockburn

Knowing what we know now in regards to omnipresence, we understand from Scripture that God is all the time, everywhere Presence. Therefore, He is always with us. In fact, He is always with everyone – believers and unbelievers alike. People from every kindred, tribe and tongue are never (*never*) out of His Presence. Nobody is - *ever*. To be even more specific about it, there is nothing on earth that takes place outside of or beyond God's Divine

PONDERING(S)

Presence. If that were to happen, He would not be omnipresent, or sovereign, which He most certainly is. So, the statement in Psalm 139:7 applies across all races, creeds, colors, and genders. In every era of time, on every square foot of dust on earth. In the heavenlies as well as throughout the universe. There is simply no place that God isn't. He is first and foremost Sovereign God over all. Period!

> *"He stretches out the north over empty space and hangs the earth on nothing. He wraps up the waters in His clouds, and the cloud does not burst under them. He obscures the face of the full moon and spreads His cloud over it. He has inscribed a circle on the surface of the waters at the boundary of light and darkness. The pillars of heaven tremble and are amazed at His rebuke.*
> *He quieted the sea with His power, and by His understanding He shattered Rahab. By His breath the heavens are cleared; His hand has pierced the fleeing serpent. Behold these are the fringes of His ways; and how faint a word we hear of Him! But His mighty thunder, who can understand?"*
> ~Job 26:7-14
> (NASB)

> *"The heavens are telling of the glory of God; and their expanse is declaring the work of His hands."*
> ~Psalm 19:1
> (NASB)

> *"For since the creation of the world His invisible attributes, His eternal power and divine nature,*

have been clearly seen, being understood through what has been made, so that they are without excuse."

~Romans 1:20
(NASB)

Present Yes, Apparent No:

"I cannot imagine how religious persons can live satisfied without the practice of the Presence of God. For my part I keep myself retired with Him in the depth and center of my soul as much as I can."

~Brother Lawrence

I've been building a case from Scripture to try and explain how I understand the development of what I'd call the theology of omnipresence. I began by tracing its evolution from the first stages of intimate relationship between the Creator and the human subjects of His creation. From there, I moved on to Moses' powerful prayer for Presence, and then on to examples from biblical history of how an understanding of Presence here on earth increased over time. Continuing in Psalms 139 and then linking David's prophetic revelation(s) to some New Testament passages which help to establish us today under the New Covenant along with that of the Old Covenant. My overall goal has been to try and show how an awareness of Jehovah's everywhere-Presence transitioned from The Garden to where we find ourselves today.

There is one more dynamic I want to unpack for you regarding the subject of Presence. That is the difference between God's manifested Presence and His supernatural abiding Presence.

For the purpose of developing that concept, I'll use

three portions of Scripture: Matthew 28:20, 1 Corinthians 3:16 and Romans 8:38-39.

In the passages I've previously mentioned from the Old Testament in this chapter, every text has been spoken more or less prophetically by those with a revelation concerning Jehovah's manifested Presence. Now I want to look at Presence using language spoken by Jesus Himself and then by Paul under the influence of the Holy Ghost.

An Axiom: Revelation to Transformation to Impartation

In Matthew 28:20, Jesus tells this to twelve of His many disciples at the end of the so-called "Great Commission." He says, *"I am with you always, even to the end of the age."* He's stating one thing directly to them while they can see, touch, and hear Him. He's also saying something that (at that moment) they didn't understand. In preparation for His death, burial, resurrection, and ascension, He is telling them that even when they can no longer have direct contact with Him in His natural physical form, He will still be available to them in a supernatural form relationally through the coming of the Spirit.

The promise which Jesus gave to the twelve, that He would always be with them in verse 20 of Matthew 28, is validated by the comments He made to them regarding the impartation and indwelling Presence of the Holy Ghost. In fact, Christ tells them it is better that He goes away in order for the Spirit to come and abide.

> *"But I tell you the truth, it is to your advantage that I go away; for if I do not go away, the Helper will not come to you; but if I go, I will send Him to you."*
>
> ~John 16:7

Such abiding speaks of the personage of the Spirit entering into the lives of believers in order to accomplish what only He can do. This *inner residence* of the Spirit makes the outward manifestations possible - which in turn testifies to the Presence of the Lord being in and with His people.

The theology related to the Holy Spirit is a vast topic to consider, which I am not going to attempt to address here. I would be barely qualified to attempt such a thing. Remember to keep in mind that my focus is still on Presence, which cannot be understood properly without bringing the third person of the Trinity into this narrative.

Here's what I'm getting at: God has moved since The Garden to re-establish Himself in an intimate relationship with humankind. That process continued through the Old Testament into the New Testament through the coming of Jesus. The bridge between the Father and the Son (in terms of relational Presence) creates a link for all those who'll accept Christ as their Savior to a personal relationship with the Godhead. The promised Holy Spirit provides the bridge for internal-supernatural-Presence to enter into the lives of those who are "born again."

Paul's statement regarding the indwelling Spirit of the Lord clearly shows us where the Presence is today:

> *"Do you not know that you are a temple of God and that the Spirit of God dwells in you?"*
> ~1 Corinthians 3:16

The Holy Spirit is resident in those who receive Him. He is actively working in and through the lives of those who are yielded to His will and His ways. In a very real sense you could say that is exactly why He is here - to establish, develop, and nurture an intimate relationship between God's people and the Trinity.

PONDERING(S)

There are two sources I'd encourage you to consult which can provide you with considerable insight into the workings of the Spirit in and through the lives of believers. Both are available online in PDF form. One is *The Presence and Work of The Holy Spirit* by R. A. Torrey. The other is The *Most Important Person On Earth* by Myles Munroe.

Paul gives us his personal perspective as to what the nature of his relationship to abiding Presence is when he says:

"I'm absolutely convinced that nothing—nothing living or dead, angelic or demonic, today or tomorrow, high or low, thinkable or unthinkable—absolutely nothing can get between us and God's love because of the way that Jesus our Master has embraced us."

~Romans 8:38-39
(The Message)

Up to this point in this chapter I've been explaining how I've seen Presence after The Fall all the way to the present. I began by working through the original breakdown in the intimate relationship between Jehovah and the first two people who had entered into personal with their God. From there, I've traced the interaction transition of the theology of omnipresence from its inception up to Paul's comments regarding the indwelling Presence embodied in the person of the Holy Ghost – the most important person on earth. Having done that, I now have a quandary to place before you in regards to how the contemporary church seems to view Presence today.

Awareness of Divine Presence:

"Our real problem, in failing to center down, is not a lack of time; it is, I fear, in too many of us, lack

PRESENCE

of joyful, enthusiastic delight in Him, lack of deep, deep-drawing love directed toward Him at every hour of the day and night."

~T. Kelly

We've been considering in some detail the biblical aspects of two key things in this chapter: the evolution of a theology of omnipresence, and the impartation of God's indwelling and abiding supernatural Presence in the lives of those who have or will receive it. The scriptural bedrock for my formulations has come from Psalm 139:7-12; Romans 8:38-39; 1 Corinthians 3:16. Those passages, taken from the Old Testament writings as well as the New, present us with a clearly established basis for stating that God is present, everywhere, all the time. He is, after all, The Great I Am (Exodus 3:14)! He always has been, and He always will be. If that is the case, made evident from the Bible, then a question arises that I must put forth. It has to do with how so many contemporary Christians understand and relate to the Presence of God living in, and moving through them. The question is this: Why do we now think we have to be somewhere specifically, or do something specifically in order to be in His Presence?

Simply stated, Scripture tells us that He is *"an ever-present help"* (Psalm 46:1). Either He is, or He isn't. Since we know that the Word of God is the embodiment of Kingdom truth, "on earth as it is in heaven" (Matthew 6:9), some believers must have a limited understanding or an inaccurate interpretation of what omnipresence means and how they should be impacted by that concept.

Watch this: Jeremiah is speaking prophetically for Jehovah when he says:

PONDERING(S)

"You will seek Me and find Me when you search for Me with all your heart."

~Jeremiah 29:13
(NASB)

Then John 4:23 tells us that God is seeking for true worshipers. So, on one hand we're being told that if we seek for His Presence, He will let us find Him. On the other hand, we're also told that if we are truly seeking Him as worshipers, then He will find us - for *"such the Father seeks."* Clearly, at least to me, Jehovah had no intention of hiding Himself from those who sought after Him, before Christ was born – according to Jeremiah. John reinforces the idea of God's Presence being available to all who are seeking to be with Him (through redemption and intimate relationship) by telling us that true worshipers are (in fact) who God is on the lookout for.

Let the Scripture speak to this once more:

"Where can I go from Your Spirit?"

~Psalm 139:7a

The answer is…nowhere!

I am convinced that the point of view that stands counter to what the Word tells us about God's manifesting, abiding, and indwelling Presence has its roots not in our belief and adherence to the truth(s) of Scripture. Rather, at issue here is our inability to remain actively aware of Presence on a regular and ongoing basis. In other words, we don't live our lives owning what we say we believe by faith. Our mental appropriation (our cognitive capacity) doesn't hold on to the biblical principle of omnipresence as we know we should. The idea of God's ever-present-ness simply leaks out due to lack of spiritual discipline, life's daily struggles and circumstances, or the deceptive tactics of the enemy of our souls. Or, perhaps it's a combination of all those things.

I'll use a couple of examples to better highlight what seems to be taking place among us. Before I do, please read again Moses' prayer in Exodus 33:13-16 - it's very important.

When we say, or sing, Lord, we won't to be in Your Presence, why do we do so? That wording sends a mixed signal doesn't it? Wouldn't it be biblically accurate to say, we're glad to be in Your Presence? Said that way, we'd be acknowledging that we are in His Presence instead of saying that something needs to take place – on our part, or on God's part – in order for His Presence to "show up."

Another example I'll use comes from an opening phrase that begins a contemporary song of praise that some churches sing. It begins by saying, "We wait for You to walk in the room." I love the song. We sing it in our fellowship. But, we've dropped that line. Why? Because it's incorrect in its theological implication. We don't wait for God to show up anywhere. He's already there before we are. That's what omnipresence means, and that's what David's revelation acknowledges in Psalm 139.

I'll place an important disclaimer here: I'm not trying to throw the baby out with the bathwater by suggesting that we re-write hundreds of songs, re-print too many books to count, and alter our teaching/preaching content to suit the comments I'm presenting. What I'm doing is sharing my personal ponderings in that regard. How you sort this all out is between you, those you're in a spiritual relationship with, and the Holy Ghost. Don't shoot me, I'm only a messenger. I'm just sayin.'

PONDERING(S)

What I think should happen is that we need to re-boot our thinking so that we better integrate an awareness of Presence into our consciousness. Doing that requires a readjustment in our thinking - that's all. The outworking (over time) is up to the Spirit to direct in accordance to the perfect will of our ever-present God.

"Why do some persons 'find' God in a way that others do not? Why does God manifest His Presence to some and let multitudes of others struggle along in the half-light of imperfect Christian experience? Of course the will of God is the same for all. He has no favorites within His household. All He has ever done for any of His children, He will do for all of His children. The difference lies not with God but with us." (A. W. Tozer)

Perhaps you know the song, "Holy Spirit." It's very popular in churches all over the globe. In fact, it has some of the most theologically solid lyrics I've heard in years, perhaps decades. The closing lines state very clearly exactly what I've been addressing in this chapter.

> *"Let us become more aware of Your Presence,*
> *Let us experience the glory of Your goodness."*
> ~Bryan and Katie Torwalt

Almighty God has chosen to impart His indwelling and manifesting Presence to those who will receive Him. He's done so in order for everyone who accepts Him to enter into an intimate relationship with the Trinity (Father, Son, and Holy Ghost). That in turn provides a way for the Spirit to teach converts (John 14:26) how to become worshipers of the One True God (Deuteronomy 5:7) in "spirit and in truth" (John 4:23). As we grow in our understanding of how to live a lifestyle of covenantal consecration, we are then equipped to serve the Lord as His witnesses (Acts 1:8), by giving testimony to who He is in our lives. In doing so, we become pro-active in our role as ambassadors for Christ, extending the gift of reconciliation to all those who will come into the Kingdom (2 Corinthians 5:18-21).

> *"For I am not ashamed of the gospel, for it is the gospel of God for salvation to everyone who believes…"*
>
> ~Romans 1:16
> (NASB)

PONDERING(S)

All His Heart

For God so loved this wicked world
He gave His only Son
So all that would believe in Him
Could have eternal life

And all it took was all His heart
But He gave it all
All it took was all His heart
Still He gave it all for us

Father, Son and Holy Ghost
We pray Thy Kingdom come
Father, Son and Holy Ghost
We pray Thy Kingdom come
As it is 'round Your throne

We worship You Lord for all that You are
For the gift that You gave in Christ
And we bow down to You in awe and wonder
God of glory, Lord of life

(W. Berry, See and Say Songs, BMI)

PRESENCE

*"Jesus the very thought of Thee
with sweetness fills my breast
But sweeter far Thy face to see
and in Thy Presence rest."*

~Bernard of Clairvaux

CHAPTER 4
Pondering Discipleship

"And even when I am old and gray, O God, do not forsake me, until I declare Your strength to this generation, Your power to all who are to come."

~Psalm 71:18
(NASB)

I live that verse. I started going gray when I was around 18 or thereabouts. So I can take some degree of ownership – a vested interest of a sort. But, I value it for another reason with considerably more attachment. I've been putting it into practice for almost 40 years. Verses like the one above take on a much deeper and more urgent meaning once you've lived it out over several decades. Having just recently entered my 70th year, my experiences with the principles and precepts of discipleship have grown into a fairly long list. One of the advantages of aging, in terms of Kingdom service, is that you gain the ability over time to be able to look further back over your shoulder than those younger than you. That's a real asset when you are attempting to disciple the generations coming up behind you. That's the reason that the scriptural directive regarding the joining of the generations retains such an important place in my life. It has for quite a spell.

There's another passage that I'll include here, because it speaks to the topic of this chapter in a profound way. Psalm 78:5-7 says:

> *"He planted a witness in Jacob, set His Word firmly in Israel, then commanded our parents to teach it to their children so the next generation would know, and all the generations to come know the truth and tell the stories so their children can trust in God, never forget the works of God but keep His commands to the letter."*
>
> (The Message)

Some of us old schoolers are still working it. We have a biblical mandate directly from Scripture to try our best to fulfill. This manuscript is part of that mandate.

> *"God doesn't come and go. God lasts. He's Creator of all you can see or imagine. He doesn't get tired out, doesn't pause to catch His breath. And He knows everything, inside and out. He energizes those who get tired, gives fresh strength to dropouts. For even young people tire and drop out, young folk in their prime stumble and fall. But those who wait upon God get fresh strength. They spread their wings and soar like eagles, they run and don't get tired, they walk and don't lag behind."*
>
> ~Isaiah 40:28-31
> (The Message)

> *"Every generation demands a demonstration of the church of Jesus Christ, relevant to its time."*
>
> ~Urban Hope

PONDERING(S)

Now that I've got that out of my system, I'll move along. Please try not to rush me.

Having made it to here in your reading, I compliment you. I trust the sojourning that's brought you this far has been worth the time and effort. I had given some thought to trying to find someone who could develop an app in order for folks to decipher "Wayne-Speak," but I abandoned that idea. Then I considered providing a link to the purchase of a decoder ring, but I gave up on that as well. I knew the Gen Xer's and the Millennials would have no idea what such a thing was. So, you've been reading at your own risk. Now, just keep pressin' ahead for a little further.

Since you're still with me I have a few words to say to you as encouragement. For some reason, the Holy Ghost has linked you and me together through the pages of this manuscript. So, it is not by chance that you're reading it. There is no such thing as chance in matters of God's Kingdom. Divine happenstance perhaps, but chance – *nada*.

> *"And we know that God causes all things to work together for good to those who love God, to those who are called according to His purpose."*
> ~Romans 8:28
> (NASB)

As I stated in the preface of this work, my intention has been to try and document my thoughts here on these pages so they would be available as a "sacrificial offering" for the Lord to use as He sees fit. I have no interest in trying to convince you to accept/believe anything I've written. Rather, I've tried to present some things to you for consideration in your own growth as a believer, or for your potential growth if/when you come to accept Christ as your Savior – the "hope of glory." (Colossians 1:27)

Some 25+ years ago, a book was published entitled, *This Present Darkness* that Christians all over the world were reading. The author Frank Peretti spoke at the church I was attending at the time, about a year or so after it came out. He told a story about something that took place between himself and the Holy Spirit which seems appropriate to share here.

He was in his study, sitting at his desk (as I recall), musing to himself, when this thought crossed his mind. "I've sold almost 750,000 copies of my book." At that moment the Spirit spoke to him and said, "Frank, you've written one. You've had nothing to do with how many books have been sold." As was the case with Frank, I've written one.

> *"We teach in a spirit of profound common sense so that we can bring each person to maturity. To be mature is to be basic. Christ! No more, no less. That's what I'm working so hard at day after day, year after year, doing my best with the energy God so graciously give me."*
>
> ~Colossians 1:28
> (The Message)

Before I get into this subject of discipleship any further, I feel I need to stress this point one last time. The point of this manuscript isn't for me to persuade you to agree with what I'm sharing. How you process my ponderings is between you and the Holy Ghost. My purpose in trying to convey the things I am is to state my thoughts as clearly as possible. Any revelation or insight that you may garner will have little to do with what I personally believe. How your belief system evolves will be based on how you sort through the things the Lord places in your path. Beyond that, I have no control over how what you're reading here will affect your life, your theology, and your relationship to God's Kingdom.

Discipleship (What it is):

I'll begin much in the same way I have in the previous chapters, by defining language and how it applies to specific words or concepts. In order to do that, the first thing to do is define the word *disciple* based on its common usages culturally and biblically.

Webster's defines a *disciple* as one who accepts and assists in spreading the doctrines of another; a convinced adherent of a school or individual. Strong's concordance defines it as a learner or pupil.

There is a perspective, which is misleading, regarding how Christians understand some of the language used in the Bible. They tend to read the Bible in a context which appears to make every word in the Bible have a religious or spiritual meaning or intent. However, that is not the case. In both the Old and New Testaments, some of the wording that's presented has been taken from the culture in which it was being spoken. In other words, all the wording isn't specifically intended to carry a meaning just for reasons of religion. Some words certainly are meant to take on a spiritual intent when they are used in a spiritual context, but that doesn't mean that the words themselves are spiritual in nature. The word *disciple* is a perfect example of that. Let me explain it this way:

Within the culture that the New Testament was written there were teachers who taught on many different subjects and beliefs. Those teachers had followers, or if you will, students who studied under their teaching. The concept of being a disciple was based on the role of a student learning under the tutoring of a qualified teacher. Think of that dynamic as applying to a classroom setting. There were students, and there were teachers. Based on the language of the day, the students would have been referred to as disciples, and the teachers would have been their disciplers. The word *disciple* is found in Scripture, but the word *discipler* isn't. Nonetheless, it is implied anytime the word *disciple* is used because in order to be a disciple there has to be someone who is discipling their students. Also, just so you'll know, the word *discipleship* isn't in the Bible either. However, the role that a teacher (rabbi) would have fulfilled in biblical times, would have been to educate his disciples in the ways that they would have had to learn in order to follow in the process of being discipled. That process would be called *discipleship*.

There's another aspect to how Christians understand the use of the term *disciple*, because of how such a word (or role) is viewed from within the church-at-large. Many believers think that when the word *disciple* is used it is referring to the twelve disciples of Jesus. But, according to Scripture, that is clearly not the case. If the word *disciple* is used to specifically relate to one (or all) of the twelve, then that is an appropriate interpretation. However, Jesus had many more disciples than the twelve we normally think of when the term is used. If you'll read Luke 6 for example, you'll find that He *"called His disciples to Him and chose twelve of them"* (v.13). Thereafter, after choosing the twelve from among an unknown number of His disciples, He then moved down the mountainside to where *"there was a large crowd of His disciples"* (v.17). Here we see Jesus first choosing His twelve from a group of disciples, and then His twelve, along with the group of disciples that the twelve were chosen from, joining together to regather with an even larger group of disciples. The picture presented here shows us that Jesus as Rabbi (teacher) had a group of disciples (students) who were following His teaching - which is why and how they became known as His disciples. There is nowhere in Scripture where Jesus is credited with giving His disciples the name (or designation) of disciple. That title would have been conveyed to them through an understanding of how the word *disciple* was used within the culture at the time that Scripture was documenting what was taking place.

Without the background I've just stated, it is very hard to interpret the true role of a disciple in Scripture. Which in turn makes it even harder to understand the role (and the term) in the times we live in currently. Hence, some theological misunderstanding has taken place over many years of misappropriation of the language we're presented with from Scripture.

Now, let's proceed to the core intention (heartbeat) of this chapter by looking at how the position of a disciple today could perhaps be re-focused with a view toward a sounder biblically-based implementation.

Based on what I've just shared, I must make one more point of clarification regarding language as to how it's used - sometimes properly, and sometimes not.

Discipleship (What it's not):

As I've stated, the biblical definition of *disciple* is a very simple one – a student (being taught by a teacher). The process in which that teaching takes place is called *discipleship*. For Christians, that is a proper use of the term for a student (disciple), and also the term for how a student is trained or educated (discipleship). However, there is another cultural term that has distorted the entire concept by substituting a word that is really only appropriate for use within a secular business or educational community. That word is *mentor*, or perhaps *mentorship*. Note please how that word is defined in Webster's, and note also where it originated.

Mentor: A friend of Odysseus entrusted with the education of Odysseus' son Telemachus. A trusted counselor or guide; a tutor or coach.

The use of that term as a substitute for discipleship is not only unbiblical, it is also misleading in terms of its theological misappropriation. That's all I'll say about that.

For me, the subject of discipleship and the role of both a disciple (student) and a teacher (disciple) has a backstory which led me to what I'm about to share next. The story is still unfolding as a work-in-progress. Here's where I've come to so far.

The story begins in John 8:31-32 which reads:

> *"So Jesus was saying to those Jews who had believed Him, 'If you continue in My word, then you are truly disciples of Mine; and you will know the truth, and the truth will make you free.'"*

Perhaps as far back as 20 years, I began sorting out that verse. I wasn't struggling with it, I just kept coming across it from time to time as I read and studied the Bible. I had the sense that the Lord was speaking to me through it, but I didn't exactly know how or why. Then, about 10 years ago, I started looking at it with more attention. As I did, this is what I saw:

I noticed that Jesus was the one who was speaking. The Jews mentioned in the text had done nothing to engage

PONDERING(S)

Him in a conversation. In other words, Jesus had something to say to them that they hadn't brought up to Him for discussion. So, what He said was important enough for Him to bring it to their attention.

Then I noticed that the Jews mentioned were believers. I researched the word believed and found that it was the same word as believe in John 3:16 and in other passages as well. The use of that word (in that context) wasn't saying that these particular Jews were coming to Jesus based on some aspect of mental interest or speculation. No, they had accepted Him as their Messiah – they were Kingdom converts. Finding that out heightened my interest in the text considerably.

Following that, I saw the placement of conditional words. Words that were either spoken, or implied as parenthetical. I started reading the passage this way:

"(If) you continue in My word, (then) you are truly disciples of Mine; and (then) you will know the truth, and (then) the truth will make you free." New light was now being shed on the verse that had been drawing me into itself for nearly two decades.

In light of that expanding illumination, I approached the verses from the perspective of what might have been the motivation for Jesus to make such a statement to believers who hadn't so much as asked anything about what He was saying. His comments were of His own doing. I assumed that He was trying to inform them of something that had to do with their relationship with Him that they had no idea of. It appeared to me that He was drawing them into a deeper aspect of intimacy that somehow went beyond merely being a believer.

At that point in my pondering, the Holy Ghost drew me directly back to the first two portions of verse 31. Christ had introduced a concept to these Jewish believers with a conditional word, meaning that they had a choice in regards to what He was about to say to them. He said, (if) they would keep His word, (then) He would consider them to truly be His disciples. Jesus was clearly saying to these converts that there was a deeper place, another level, beyond where they currently were in their understanding and in their relationship to Him, and the things related to being His followers.

In Wayne-Speak the implication of His words was this: 'You believe in Me, and that's all well and good. But, there is a way of being with Me that you can take part in. However, to do so you will have to keep My word – obey what I tell you, follow My lead, yield to Me as *Savior and Lord* as you seek to know and fulfill My Father's will.' Then, following those stunning words, He goes on to tell them that if they will do that, two more things will take place in their lives as believers.

1. They will come to know the truth
2. Truth will set them free (freer that they already were by believing in Him)

In essence the Lord seemed to be saying:

{You can be a believer without being a disciple, but you can't be a disciple without first being a believer.}

After coming to a point of understanding which had taken years to arrive at, I accepted the fact that (according to Scripture) there are two distinctions, or roles, available through salvation in Christ Jesus. One is that of being a believer. The other is that of being a disciple. Having that settled in my head, I figured that was a perspective to carry and sort out for the rest of my life. However, that wasn't the end of the journey. It turned out to only be the beginning.

I began to notice that I rarely (if ever) heard this concept mentioned as it related to our lives in Kingdom service to Christ Jesus. I knew of no teachings or published works regarding what I believed that John 8:31-32 said, nor was I aware of any sermons which addressed this topic of believers and disciples. I decided the less said the better since the subject seemed to be one that I was perhaps misunderstanding entirely. And, then, *Bam!* a book by Dallas Willard entitled *The Great Omission* ended up in my lap. That's when this entire process got very interesting.

The premise of Willard's work in that book gave me a broader context in which to consider this business of believers and disciples. Very simply and briefly the overview is this:

Christ fulfilled two key roles while He was here on earth. He was the Messiah, the Savior of humankind. He was also a Rabbi. His Messianic role was accepted by those who gave their lives to Him as their Redeemer. The other role (that of Rabbi) was accepted within the culture of His day by everyone who knew Him to be a knowledgeable and qualified teacher, and also by those who decided to follow Him - by becoming His disciples – which is exactly what John 8:31-32 speaks to. Willard addressed this issue by titling his book, *The Great Omission*. Here's what he meant by that:

The contemporary church of today accepts Christ as their Lord, and thereby enters into eternal life through the saving work of the Lord, receiving the promise of heaven and home. However, the acceptance of Jesus as Rabbi (teacher/discipler) is no longer as important as it once was. At least not from a biblically theological perspective. Why?

Because for believers to accept Christ as their Rabbi, that would place them in the role of being a student (disciple) directly under His charge as their teacher. By doing so, they would then have to not only study and relate to what He teaches, they would then have to put into practice the things that they are being taught. That process in and of itself has no real bearing on salvation, so consequently it has become an option in terms of how believers live out their lives in an intimate relationship of worship and service to their Savior and Lord. That is, as Willard calls it, the great omission! Accepting Jesus as Savior, but (in a sense) rejecting Him as Teacher. Which in turn makes becoming a disciple a non-essential in terms of how we as Christians live our lives.

Having read that, I now knew that there was at least one other person - considerably more knowledgeable than I – who related to this believer/disciple subject the way I did. If I was way off target about this, I knew I wasn't the only one.

Then this happened…

The "Great Commission"

About three years ago, I was in intercession for the nations (Psalm 2:8) when I began to pose a prayer to the Father. The prayer question was, "Lord, why is the charge of the so-called 'Great Commission' taking so long to be fulfilled?" When I prayed that, in my spirit I heard the Holy Ghost say, "Consider John 8:31 and 32." I was stunned! From there the interchange that took place turned into a profound moment in my life.

I said, "What does the John 8 passage have to do with Matthew 28:18-21?" The Spirt said, "Who did Jesus give the charge of the 'Great Commission' to?"

PONDERING(S)

As I re-read the passage I noted that Christ had spoken it directly to His disciples. At that moment, the Spirit answered my original question by saying, "The reason that the 'Great Commission' is taking so long to be fulfilled is that there are too few disciples available to get the job done."

I was undone, overwhelmed, broken, and astounded. Up until that moment, I had understood / believed that the words Jesus had spoken in Matthew 28:18-20 were directed to and intended for the body of Christ at large. I no longer believe that to be the case. The only people present when the "Great Commission" was spoken were His disciples and their Lord.

> *"But the eleven disciples proceeded to Galilee, to the mountain which Jesus had designated. When they saw Him, they worshiped Him; but some were doubtful. And Jesus came up and spoke to them, saying, 'All authority has been given to Me in heaven and on earth. Go therefore and make disciples of all the nations, baptizing them in the name of the Father and the Son and the Holy Spirit, teaching them to observe all that I commanded you; and lo, I am with you always, even to the end of the age."*
>
> ~Matthew 28:16-20
> (NASB)

The links between John 8:31 and 32 to the writings of Dallas Willard in *The Great Omission* and then on to the words Jesus spoke directly and specifically to His disciples in Matthew 28:16-20 had all fallen into place. The Holy Ghost answered my question regarding the fulfillment of the charge Christ gave. He (the Spirit) also opened up an entirely different way of viewing the roles of believers and disciples.

My comments are not intended with a view toward some sort of class system among "born again" believers and disciples. There is no condescension contained in my remarks. One role is not above the other. There is no over/under position reference in Scripture, nor am I making any such claims. I am merely pointing out what I understand the passages I've mentioned to be saying. I am also explaining what has taken place in my belief system through my interchanges with God's Word, and the moving of the Holy Ghost in my relationship with Him.

My bottom line is this: Jesus made a distinction between believers and disciples in John 8:31-32. Jesus spoke the so called "Great Commission" to His disciples. He didn't do so by first separating or dismissing those who believed in Him. However, there is no mention of believers being present when the charge to the disciples to go make other disciples was spoken. That's because believers can't disciple others into becoming disciples. Only those who have been discipled by their teacher (Rabbi) are qualified and equipped to do that. As I said earlier, you can be a believer without being a disciple, but you can't be a disciple without first being a believer. That in turn, brings us full circle and returns us to the John 8 and 31 and 32 in Jesus' own words to believers. The key that unlocks each of those doors is, "If you keep my word," not, "Are you saved?" Those are two entirely different statements. One has to do with salvation, the other has to do with unconditional and obedient service. There's a term for that – it's consecration.

Pentecostal to the Present:

There is one remaining bridge to be crossed regarding

the subject of discipleship. It's found in Acts 1:8 as a link to the "Great Commission" and the role of believers and disciples.

> *"You will receive power when the Holy Spirit has come upon you; and you shall be My witnesses both in Jerusalem, and in all Judea and Samaria, and even to the remotest part of the earth."*
>
> ~Acts 1:8
> (NASB)

As was the case when Jesus gave His charge to "go and make disciples" to the eleven disciples who were with Him, so also the comments (the directives) of Acts 1:8 are spoken to disciples. I'll address how the impartation of Acts 1:8 applies to *all* Christians shortly. But, for now just consider what I'm about to say in the context of what was taking place just prior to Pentecost among disciples only. Why? Because no believers are mentioned in that verse, so we are given no record that believers were in attendance. Nothing tells us that they were excluded for any reason. However, there is no record of anyone being present to receive what was spoken except for disciples.

You may recall that in the last chapter focused on Presence, I mentioned a protocol for how a theology of omnipresence evolved from the answer to Moses' prayer in Exodus 33:13-17. Now, apply that protocol to the Acts 1:8 unfolding.

The passage clearly states that the Power of the Spirit to accomplish what's necessary to fulfill the charge being given is proceeded by the impartation of Presence. *"You shall receive power (after) the Holy Ghost has come."* The verse goes on to say what will happen thereafter. Once empowered by the Spirit (after Presence has come), the disciples would become witnesses. The text doesn't say that they will go and do witnessing. It says that they will become witnesses themselves. Their lives will be transformed by the indwelling power of the Spirit through the internal Presence abiding inside of them.

That is exactly what Moses prayed for, and that is exactly how Jehovah said He would answer Moses' prayer!

The prayer of Exodus 33:13-17 was that God's Presence would go with His people so that they would be known (set apart) through such Presence in order that anyone and everyone they would come in contact with would know that they were in fact God's chosen people (1 Peter 2:9). Moses stated that just having God's living Presence would be enough to "distinguish" them from those who didn't know the One True God. He didn't say that God's people would have to *do* anything. He said they would only have to show up with God's Presence abiding in and among them. Doing so, would in turn make them witnesses - which is what Act 1:8 says would happen to the disciples in order for them to carry out the remaining directive of that verse. They were to go out into the regions of the world as witnesses and make proclamation through their testimony, which produces Kingdom expansion as conversions took place. Then, once souls had been redeemed through the saving grace of God working through the drawing of the Spirit, the ability for the disciples to then make disciples would be possible.

The cycle of answered prayer for Presence which began in the interchange between Moses and Jehovah continued all the way to the charge of the "Great Commission." Which in turn is directly linked to the charge of the pre-Pentecost directives of Acts 1:8. And the outworking of the Acts 1:8 mandate (for all intents and purposes) falls directly in line with Moses' requests and Jesus' statement to His disciples in Matthew 28:16-20. The *"Go ye"* (KJV) is the call that was given. That call began with Moses' prayer, and then finds its way into the ears (and hearts) of the disciples - both then and now. That process brings us to how it applies to ALL believers living today, and those believers who are yet to be "born again" into active service for the expansion of God's Kingdom.

DISCIPLESHIP

SPLENDOR

The charity of God's Spirit,
Is a gift beyond all measure
It's a treasure
That can't be bought or sold
The Divine intervention of His Presence moving among us
Creates a world of wonders to behold

Encounters in His Kingdom,
For those with eyes to see them
Are expressions of a life meant to be shared

Like an ever-flowing fountain,
Running down from off Mount Zion
Freely flowing out to everywhere

Still You move, on the wind, over and over again
Still You move in splendor

The clarity of purpose, manifest through grace, through mercy
Can be measured day to day without end
As the hope sent down from heaven,
Touches every generation
The cycle is repeated once again

Still You move, on the wind, over and over again
Still You move in splendor

(W. Berry, See and Say Songs, BMI)

The Son asked the Father to send the Spirit to teach converts (John 14:26) how to become worshipers of the One True God (Deuteronomy 5:7) in "spirit and in truth" (John 4:23). As we grow in our understanding of how to live a lifestyle of covenantal consecration, we are then equipped to serve the Lord as His witnesses (Acts 1:8), by giving testimony to who He is in our lives. In doing so, we become pro-active in our role as ambassadors for Christ, extending the gift of reconciliation to all those who will be added to the church in order to advance the Kingdom (2 Corinthians 5:18-21).

The Big If:

> *"Life is meant to be lived from a Center, a Divine Center. Each one of us can live such a life of amazing power, peace and serenity of integration and confidence and simplified multiplicity, on one condition - that is, if we really want to."*
>
> ~T. Kelly

> *"If you keep my word..."*
>
> ~John 8:31-32

In the KJV translation that phrase reads, "if you continue in my word." The word *continue* in the Greek is *meno*, meaning to stay (in a given place, relation or state of expectancy); to abide, dwell, endure, be present, remain, tarry (for or with). If that doesn't speak directly to an intimate relationship to Presence, then I don't know what does.

The qualifier for becoming a disciple is the keeping of God's word. Not belief in Jesus Christ as the Messiah. Not being "born again." Not good works, or the ability to perform "signs and wonders." Not evangelism. Not soul winning. Not mission work, or church planting. Living a lifestyle that testifies to obedient service by keeping God's word is the condition put forth in John 8:31 for being a disciple of the Lord Jesus. How we understand, relate to, and embrace that one short phrase of Scripture is the determining factor for living as a disciple. The charge of the so called "Great Commission" is incorporated into such a keeping of the Word. So is the empowerment imparted (to the disciples) in Acts 1:8. The going forth in order to make disciples is charged to those who are first disciples themselves.

> *"And do not be conformed to this world, but be transformed by the renewing of your mind, so that you may prove what the will of God is, that which is good and acceptable and perfect."*
>
> ~Romans 12:2
> (NASB)

> *"The unspiritual self, just as it is by nature, can't receive the gifts of God's Spirit. There's no capacity for them. They seem like so much silliness. Spirit can be known only by spirit – God's Spirit and our spirits in open communion. Spiritually alive, we have access to everything God's Spirit is doing, and can't be judged by unspiritual critics. Isaiah's question, 'Is there anyone around who knows God's Spirit, anyone who knows what He is doing?' has been answered: Christ knows, and we have Christ's Spirit."*
>
> ~1 Corinthians 2:14-16
> (The Message)

PONDERING(S)

RENEW MY MIND

Sometimes I'm feelin' down so low,
I just can't face the day
The tempter's turned my heart so cold,
and heaven seems so far away
But then I see where I've gone wrong,
I've strayed away from You too long
I long to be where I belong,
so down on my knees I pray
Heavenly Father, help me find my way
CHORUS:
Father, renew my mind
set my thoughts in the heavenlies
Father, I've been so blind,
now I need the touch of Your hands on me
Father, open up my eyes,
let me see what You are doing
I'm willin' just to be a part,
of how Your Holy Spirit is moving
Father, renew my mind,
Father, renew my mind
Heavenly Father, renew my mind

As a child of God I'm called to live,
a life of love and grace
To give all that I've got to give,
until I behold His face
But, sometimes sin takes hold of me,
it won't let go, and I can't get free
But my sweet Savior rescues me,
and every demon has to run
At the power in the name of God's Son
REPEAT CHORUS:

(W. Berry, See and Say Songs, BMI)

DISCIPLESHIP

Some say that the organized church is in decline in America. That may be the case, but, I know from personal experiences (12 years of ministry on the continent of Africa), that it is exploding and expanding there as well as in nations all over the earth (see Psalm 2:8). Conversions into God's Kingdom are taking place in huge numbers. Belief in Christ is increasing at a steady and rapid rate. However, there continues to be a shortage of disciples in fellowships large and small. The wooing of the Spirit, drawing millions into redemption through Christ Jesus is taking place unabated. But, the call for disciples who are willing and equipped to make disciples is lacking in congregations everywhere (Matthew 28:19). Coming to terms with that reality could create perhaps the greatest display of Presence, Power, and Proclamation for the Kingdom of God that humankind has ever known. We, as God's people – the chosen and elect (I Peter 2:9) – continue to be grace-favored with the opportunity before us to see that *"the earth will be filled with the knowledge of the glory of the Lord, as the waters cover the sea"* (Habakkuk 2:14). That mandate awaits those who will hear the call, and yield themselves to it – through their ongoing acts of consecration, worship, and the empowerment of the abiding-indwelling Presence of God's Holy Spirit, going forth into *"all Judea, and Samaria, and even to the remotest part of the earth (Acts 1:8)."*

EPILOGUE

The process of consecration, and the covenant that it is built upon, is vital in the life of every believer who desires to live in obedient service to the Lord. Being available in an ongoing intimate relationship with the Father, Son, and Holy Ghost is essential if we intend to participate (rather than spectate) in any move where the manifestations of God's Kingdom are taking place. Living our lives in that fashion provides a context for becoming a *"living and holy sacrifice"* which is our *"spiritual service of worship"* (Romans 12:1, NASB).

Almighty God has chosen to impart His manifesting and indwelling Presence to those who will receive Him (John 1:12 and 13). He's done so in order for everyone who accepts Him to enter into an intimate relationship with the Trinity (Father, Son and Holy Ghost). That in turn provides a way for the Spirit to teach converts (John 14:26) how to become worshipers of the One True God (Deuteronomy 5:7) in *"spirit and in truth"* (John 4:23). As we grow in our understanding of how to live a lifestyle of covenantal consecration, we are then equipped to serve the Lord as His witnesses (Acts 1:8), by giving testimony to who He is in our lives. In doing so, we become pro-active in our role as ambassadors for Christ, extending the gift of reconciliation to all those who will come into the Kingdom (2 Corinthians 5:18-21).

Never Squander a Ponder

In Remembrance

Thomas Kelly received word on January 17, 1941 that Harper and Brothers was willing to meet with him to discuss the publication of a devotional book. He died of a heart attack later that same day. Three months later one of Kelly's colleagues submitted five of Kelly's devotional essays to the publisher along with a biographical sketch of Kelly. The book was published under the title *A Testament of Devotion*. Some of his other essays have been collected in a book entitled *The Eternal Promise*.

Also Available From

WordCrafts Press

Speaking and Hearing the Word of God
A Speech-Language Pathologist's Perspective
                              by Rodney Boyd

Morning Mist
Stories from the Water's Edge
                              by Barbie Loflin

Why I Failed in the Music Business
and how NOT to follow in my footsteps
                              by Steve Grossman

Youth Ministry is Easy!
and 9 other lies
                              by Aaron Shaver

Chronicles of a Believer
                              by Don McCain

Illuminations
                    by Paula K. Parker and Tracy Sugg

www.wordcrafts.net

www.ingramcontent.com/pod-product-compliance
Lightning Source LLC
Chambersburg PA
CBHW020618300426
44113CB00007B/692